The Kids Book of
GREAT
CANADIANS

WRITTEN BY

Elizabeth MacLeod

ILLUSTRATED BY

John Mantha

KIDS CAN PRESS

With lots of love to my wonderful nephews and nieces,
Cameron, Ceri, David, Jennifer, Laura Beth, Rachel, Tim and Tom

Acknowledgements

Writing a book such as this one made me very proud to be a Canadian. I'm grateful to Kids Can Press for giving me the opportunity to write this book and to find out so much more about the great Canadians who have made our country so wonderful. Thank you also to the many people who read parts of the manuscript and commented on it, especially David Wistow at the Art Gallery of Ontario.

Many thanks to John Mantha for bringing these great Canadians alive with his terrific paintings. Thanks also to Patricia Buckley for her photo research work and to Julia Naimska for bringing everything together so well with her design. Special thanks to Chris McClymont and Val Wyatt for editing this book and caring so much about it. Thanks to Dad, John and Douglas and, as ever, love and thanks to Paul, who is truly a great Canadian!

Many sources have been used for the information in this book but the primary sources are *The Canadian Encyclopedia* and *The Junior Encyclopedia of Canada*.

Photo Credits

Every reasonable effort has been made to trace ownership of, and give accurate credit to, copyrighted material. Information that would enable the publisher to correct any discrepancies in future editions would be appreciated.

Abbreviations

t = top; b = bottom; c = centre; l = left; r = right

All stamps copyright © Canada Post. Reproduced with permission.

p. 8: © 1992 Canada Post; **p. 16:** © 1963 Canada Post; **p. 25:** © 1981 Canada Post; **p. 35:** © 1993 Canada Post; **p. 38:** *Autumn Hillside* by Frank Carmichael/Art Gallery of Ontario, Toronto: Gift of J.S. McLean Collection. Donated by the Ontario Heritage Foundation, 1988; **p. 45:** © 1990 Canada Post; **p. 50:** © 2000 Canada Post; **p. 56:** © The Nobel Foundation; **p. 57:** (tl) © 1980 Canada Post, (tr) © 1968 Canada Post; **p. 59:** (tl) © 2000 Canada Post, (tr) © 1993 Canada Post; **p. 60:** (tr) © 2000 Canada Post, (c) © 1969 Canada Post, (b) © 1991 Canada Post.

Kids Can Press acknowledges the financial support of the Government of Ontario, through the Ontario Media Development Corporation's Ontario Book Initiative; the Ontario Arts Council; the Canada Council for the Arts; and the Government of Canada, through the BPIDP, for our publishing activity.

Published in Canada by
Kids Can Press Ltd.
29 Birch Avenue
Toronto, ON M4V 1E2

Published in the U.S. by
Kids Can Press Ltd.
2250 Military Road
Tonawanda, NY 14150

www.kidscanpress.com

Edited by Valerie Wyatt and Christine McClymont
Designed by Julia Naimska
Printed and bound in Singapore

The hardcover edition of this book is smyth sewn casebound.
The paperback edition of this book is limp sewn with a drawn-on cover.

CM 04 0 9 8 7 6 5 4 3
CM PA 08 0 9 8 7 6 5 4 3 2 1

Library and Archives Canada Cataloguing in Publication

MacLeod, Elizabeth
The kids book of great Canadians / written by Elizabeth
MacLeod ; illustrated by John Mantha.

Includes index.
For ages 8–12.

ISBN 978-1-55337-366-7 (bound). ISBN 978-1-55453-255-1 (pbk.)

1. Canada—Biography—Juvenile literature.
I. Mantha, John II. Title. III. Title: Great Canadians.

FC25.M29 2004   j971'.009'9   C2003-903376-7

Kids Can Press is a *corus*™ Entertainment company

CONTENTS

CANADIANS ARE GREAT!

Canada is the world's second-largest country, but Canadians are second to none. Some Canadians — the "greats" — stand out above the rest because of the important contributions they've made, not only to our country but also to the world. They've given us many reasons to feel proud. Courage, determination and enthusiasm make these men, women and children special.

Canadian "greats" have fought life-threatening diseases, transformed the way we communicate, or earned honours for bravery during wartime. Canadian artists have affected the way we see our nation – and how the world sees us — while Canadian athletes have amazed us all with their skills. In this book you'll read about more than 150 "greats" and their incredible accomplishments.

Some great Canadians have had an impact far beyond Canada's borders. *Alexander Graham Bell* (page 22), *Lucy Maud Montgomery* (page 32) and *Wayne Gretzky* (page 48) are known around the world. Others have made their mark at home, improving the way Canadians live. Prime Minister *Lester B. Pearson* (page 42) helped give us our maple leaf flag,

a uniquely Canadian symbol. The first woman member of Canada's parliament, *Agnes Macphail* (page 45), showed the country that women had important things to say and contributions to make.

Billy Bishop, World War I pilot (page 9)

Many great Canadians lived before Canada was a nation. During the War of 1812, *Laura Secord* (page 8) warned the soldiers defending Canada of a surprise attack by the Americans, and became legendary in Canadian history. Other "greats," such as *Rick Hansen* (page 7), who has raised money for spinal-cord research, are making their contributions right now. Take a look at the time line on page 62 and you'll see that great Canadians are spread throughout Canada's history.

Lucy Maud Montgomery, author of Anne of Green Gables *(page 32)*

Frederick Banting and Charles Best

Frederick Banting and Charles Best, discoverers of insulin (page 20)

Craig Kielburger, spokesperson for children's rights (page 7)

Josiah Henson, Black rights activist (page 10)

Pauline Johnson, poet and Native rights activist (page 36)

All Born in Canada?

Not all of the great Canadians you'll meet in this book were born here. Most of the explorers who opened the country to the fur trade and settlement were born in Europe. Many immigrants came to Canada looking for a better life. Others came looking for adventure and found a country that inspired them to work hard and make a difference. They're included in this book because they've all helped to make Canada great.

Perhaps most important are the "greats" who inspire their fellow Canadians to dream and make those dreams come true. *Terry Fox* (page 6) dreamed of running across Canada to raise money to fight cancer. Now the annual run held in his honour is the world's largest, single-day fundraising event for cancer. Canadian girls have been inspired by *Roberta Bondar*, the country's first woman astronaut (page 19), to believe that any career is open to them.

Get ready to meet Canada's greatest heroes, explorers, scientists, doctors, business people, artists, politicians, athletes and more. May their stories inspire you to be a great Canadian, too.

Young people have left their mark on Canada and the world, too. *Madeleine de Verchères* was just 14 when she defended her settlement against an attack (page 61). Children's rights activist *Craig Kielburger* began his work in 1995, at the age of 12 (page 7).

Changing Place Names

Some of the provinces and territories have changed their names during the lives of the great Canadians. In this book, the current provincial or territorial name is usually used. Here are some of the older names:

- Ontario was known as Upper Canada from 1791 to 1840 and then Canada West from 1841 to 1867.
- Quebec was New France from 1608 to 1763, the Province of Quebec from 1763 to 1791, Lower Canada from 1791 to 1840 and then Canada East from 1841 to 1867.
- Alberta and Saskatchewan were part of the Northwest Territories until 1905.
- Nunavut was part of the Northwest Territories before 1999.
- Newfoundland changed its name to Newfoundland and Labrador in 2001.

Pierre Elliott Trudeau, former prime minister of Canada (page 40)

Elizabeth Arden, cosmetics innovator (page 30)

Nancy Greene, Olympic Ski Champion (page 53)

Roberta Bondar, astronaut (page 19)

HEROES

Meet 16 incredible Canadians who have changed life in Canada and the world. Some of these heroes lived long ago, while others are still working hard today. They've fought for people's rights, battled life-threatening diseases and defended Canada against its enemies.

Although these great Canadians have worked in many different fields, they have one important thing in common: they are all ordinary people who had the courage to do something extraordinary. In doing so, they've inspired other Canadians to be heroes, too.

Terry Fox

> *Runner and fundraiser for cancer research*
>
> *Born: July 28, 1958, at Winnipeg, MB*
>
> *Died: June 28, 1981, at New Westminster, BC*

About 6 million people in nearly 60 countries take part in Terry Fox runs each year and have raised more than $400 million for cancer research. The runs are the world's largest, single-day fundraising events for cancer, and they're all thanks to one courageous hero who had a dream.

In 1977 doctors discovered that Terrance "Terry" Fox — then only 18 years old — had a rare form of bone cancer. His right leg had to be amputated above the knee. Terry became determined to do something so that other people wouldn't have to go through the same thing. He decided to run across Canada to raise money for cancer research and increase awareness of the disease. Terry called his run The Marathon of Hope.

On April 12, 1980, Terry began his incredible journey at St. John's, Newfoundland, running a distance equal to a marathon every day. He faced icy storms, blustery winds and burning heat, and he still kept running.

But on September 1, 1980, Terry's run ended in Thunder Bay, Ontario — the cancer had spread to his lungs, forcing him to stop. He died less than a year later.

"I just wish people would realize that anything is possible if you try," Terry once said. This Canadian hero realized his dream of raising one dollar from every Canadian. His Marathon of Hope united the country behind him and made Canada proud. Today the Terry Fox Foundation continues his dream of fundraising to find a cure for cancer.

"DREAMS ARE MADE IF PEOPLE ONLY TRY. I BELIEVE IN MIRACLES ... I HAVE TO ... BECAUSE SOMEWHERE THE HURTING MUST STOP."

— *Terry Fox*

Rick Hansen

Wheelchair athlete and fundraiser for spinal-cord research

Born: *Aug. 26, 1957, at Port Alberni, BC*

Richard "Rick" Hansen was a high-energy kid who loved sports. But a truck accident when he was just 15 severed his spinal cord and left his legs paralyzed. Scared and in a lot of pain, Rick was determined that he was not giving up sports. Within a few years, he had become a world-class wheelchair athlete.

Rick's friend Terry Fox inspired him to raise money for spinal-cord research and wheelchair sports. Rick decided to do it by wheelchairing

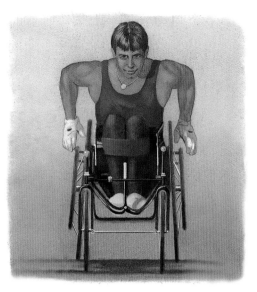

40 000 km (24 855 mi.) — a distance equal to once around the world. His Man in Motion World Tour left Vancouver in March 1985 and eventually took him across 34 countries.

During the Man in Motion tour, Rick Hansen pushed the wheels of his chair about 30 000 times a day and wore out 160 wheelchair tires.

Rick was on the road for more than two years, wheeling 50 to 70 km (30 to 45 mi.) daily. His travels took him through mountains, deserts and blinding snowstorms. When it was over, the Man in Motion tour had raised $24 million. Rick continues to promote both spinal-cord research and disabled athletes through his Rick Hansen Institute, established in 1997.

Craig Kielburger

Spokesperson for children's rights

Born: *Dec. 17, 1982, at Toronto, ON*

One morning, while searching for the comics in the daily newspaper, 12-year-old Craig Kielburger was stunned by a photo of a child labourer who had battled bad working conditions and been murdered for his protests. It made Craig wonder about kids' working conditions around the world, as well as child poverty, health and safety.

Craig and some friends founded Kids Can Free the Children, an organization to help kids everywhere. It's the world's largest network of kids helping kids and has more than 100 000 members in 35 countries.

Travelling around the world, talking with young people and meeting with countries' leaders are just some of Craig's many activities. "Young people have a great deal to contribute," says Craig. "We may not have all the answers, but we are willing to learn — there is no shortage of energy and enthusiasm."

Because of his work, Craig has been nominated for the Nobel Peace Prize (see page 56).

Isaac Brock

British commander in the War of 1812

Born: *Oct. 6, 1769, at St. Peter Port, Guernsey (part of Great Britain)*

Died: *Oct. 13, 1812, at Queenston Heights, ON*

When Isaac Brock was 15, he joined the British army. He was a brave soldier and by age 28 was made lieutenant colonel of his regiment. In 1802, as war was brewing between Britain and America, Isaac was sent to Canada. He believed that when war erupted the Americans would attack the closest British colony — Canada — especially what's now known as Ontario.

By 1807 Isaac was in command of all British forces in Canada. For the next five years, he improved defences and trained the soldiers. Because of his hard work and leadership, the colony was ready when war broke out with the Americans in 1812.

By this time, Isaac was major general in charge of Upper Canada. In July 1812, the Americans invaded at present-day Windsor, Ontario. With his outnumbered army of British, Native and Canadian soldiers, Isaac boldly pushed the Americans back and forced them to surrender. The Americans were especially afraid of the Native warriors led by Tecumseh (page 11).

Isaac's courage inspired his soldiers. When the American army crossed the Niagara River on October 13, Isaac and his troops fought them at Queenston Heights. He was shot and killed, but the Canadian soldiers fought on and won the battle. Because of his heroism, Isaac has become known as "the man who saved Canada."

Isaac Brock was buried four times — once soon after his death, a second time at the base of the monument built for him at Queenston, a third time when the monument was blown up and his body had to be moved and finally under the current Brock's Monument.

Laura Secord

Heroine of the War of 1812

Born: *Sept. 13, 1775, at Great Barrington, MA, U.S.*

Died: *Oct. 17, 1868, at Chippawa (now Niagara Falls), ON*

In 1812, the United States and Britain began a two-year battle for control of Canada. It was on June 21, 1813, that American officers forced their way into Laura Secord's house in Upper Canada (Ontario) and ordered her to give them rooms and dinner. When they thought Laura was out of earshot, they boasted of their plans to make a surprise attack on the British soldiers at Beaver Dams, about 32 km (20 mi.) away. Laura knew she must warn the British of the attack, even though she risked being shot if the Americans captured her.

The next day, the sun blazed as Laura struggled through thick forests and muddy swamps to warn the British. Two days later, thanks to her courage, 116 British and Canadian soldiers, including 70 Native soldiers, ambushed the 500 Americans and forced them to surrender.

Billy Bishop

World War I pilot

Born: *Feb. 9, 1894, at Owen Sound, ON*

Died: *Sept. 10, 1956, at Palm Beach, FL, U.S.*

While trying to free his horse from a dirty, muddy field, World War I cavalry soldier Billy Bishop looked up and saw his first airplane. He watched the plane and envied its pilot. Flying seemed so free — and clean! It wasn't long before he transferred to the Royal Flying Corps to fight for Britain and its allies (including Canada) from the air.

William "Billy" Bishop wasn't a great pilot, but practice and his incredible eyesight made him an amazing shot. He earned the Distinguished Flying Cross after scoring 25 victories in just 12 days. Before dawn on June 2, 1917, flying alone as usual, Billy attacked a German airfield and destroyed three planes. This was the first time an airplane had been used to attack a force on the ground in enemy territory.

Billy's daring raid earned him the Victoria Cross, the highest of all British honours for bravery in battle. He was the first Canadian airman to win the award.

Billy took part in more than 170 air battles during the war. Later he helped create the Royal Canadian Air Force (RCAF). And during World War II, he was made an honorary air marshal in the RCAF.

DID YOU KNOW

Billy Bishop shot down 72 enemy planes, more than any other Allied airman. In one battle, this ace brought down five planes in just five minutes.

Sam Steele

One of Canada's first Mounties

Born: *Jan. 5, 1849, at Purbrook (near today's Orillia), ON*

Died: *Jan. 30, 1919, at London, England*

Samuel Steele was only 24 when he joined the just-formed North West Mounted Police (later the Royal Canadian Mounted Police) as a sergeant major. But he was already a tough soldier. His incredible strength and endurance made everyone respect him.

Sam always seemed to be where the action was. He kept order among rowdy workers building Canada's transcontinental railway in the 1880s. While extremely ill in 1885, he stopped a railway strike without firing a shot.

In the late 1890s, Sam enforced the law among rough miners of the Klondike gold rush. He became known as the "Lion of the North." Later he fought in the South African (Boer) War and was a major general in World War I.

Sam's commitment to his country and his work have made him a legend across Canada.

Mary Ann Shadd

Black rights activist

Born: Oct. 9, 1823, at Wilmington, DE, U.S.

Died: June 5, 1893, at Washington, DC, U.S.

When Mary Ann Shadd was growing up in Delaware, she discovered that her father's shoemaking shop was a stop on the Underground Railroad. This was a secret network of people who helped enslaved Black people escape from slave states in the southern United States to freedom in northern states and Canada.

Although Mary Ann was born a free person, when she was 27 the U.S. government passed a law that meant free Black people could be sold into slavery. To avoid this fate, she and her family fled to Windsor, Canada West.

Mary Ann strongly believed that Black and White people should live together, not in separate communities. She was an experienced teacher and in 1851 set up a school for both Black and White students. Unfortunately, many White parents refused to enrol their children.

In 1853 she started a newspaper called the *Provincial Freeman* and wrote about the value of living together. The paper exposed discrimination and also reported to Americans on Black life in Canada.

It was uncommon at that time for women to speak in public, but Mary Ann was a good speaker. Dealing with hecklers was one of her special skills. Mary Ann was a crusader, always fighting for the rights of women and Black people.

Mary Ann Shadd was the first Black woman to start and run a newspaper in North America.

Josiah Henson

Founder of the Dawn Settlement

Born: June 15, 1789, at Charles County, MD, U.S.

Died: May 5, 1883, at Dresden, ON

Born a slave in Maryland, Josiah Henson was sold three times before he turned 18. At age 40, he feared that he and his wife would be sold and separated, so they fled. With the help of the Underground Railroad, they arrived in Canada in 1830. "When my feet first touched the Canadian shore," said Josiah, "I threw myself on the ground, rolled in the sand, seized handfuls of it and kissed them."

While getting used to freedom and life in Canada, Josiah helped many other enslaved people escape from the United States. Then in 1841 he helped create the Dawn Settlement at Dresden, Canada West, where he taught many Black newcomers to be successful farmers.

Josiah was likely the inspiration for the Uncle Tom character in the book *Uncle Tom's Cabin*. This novel by Harriet Beecher Stowe helped make people aware of the unfairness of slavery.

In 1983 Josiah became the first Black Canadian to be featured on a Canadian stamp — a well-deserved honour.

Adam Dollard des Ormeaux

Garrison commander of the fort at Ville-Marie

Born: 1635, probably in France

Died: May 1660, at Long Sault, PQ

By 1660 there were constant fears in Ville-Marie (now Montreal) of attack by the Iroquois, as the French and the Native people (and the British) all fought to control the fur trade. Adam Dollard des Ormeaux decided that the only chance the little settlement had was for soldiers to try to ambush the Iroquois before they got to Ville-Marie. So he took 60 French and Native people and headed up the Ottawa River to the Long Sault rapids.

There they ran into a much larger force of Iroquois, who quickly brought in 500 more warriors. Adam and his men hung on for about seven days, but all were killed. However, before they died, they injured or killed so many Iroquois that the plan to attack Ville-Marie and New France was abandoned. Adam's bravery and determination saved the lives of many French Canadians.

Tecumseh

Native leader in the War of 1812

Born: around 1768, in the Ohio Valley, U.S.

Died: Oct. 5, 1813, near Moraviantown (now Thamesville), ON

"A more ... gallant Warrior does not I believe exist," is what General Isaac Brock (page 8) wrote about Tecumseh. Brock and Tecumseh worked well together, leading their men against the Americans in the War of 1812. They admired each other's courage, daring and skill in battle.

One of the greatest leaders of the Shawnee people, Tecumseh tried to bring together various Native tribes. He felt they would have more power if they united to face the Americans,

who were trying to take over their land in the Ohio Valley. Tecumseh had his people fight on Britain's side in the War of 1812 because he thought that if the British won, they would help him defend his people's land.

Tecumseh met Brock early in the war. Together they won many critical battles, including the capture of Detroit in August 1812. But Brock was killed in battle later in 1812, and his replacement was much less courageous. At the Battle of Moraviantown, Upper Canada, in October 1813, British troops fled from the Americans, leaving Tecumseh and his 500 soldiers to face 3000 enemies. The determined chief fought bravely, but was killed in battle.

DID YOU KNOW

Tecumseh means "Panther Crossing."

The Famous Five

Today Canadian women take for granted that they can run for Parliament and be senators. But they wouldn't have these rights without the determination and dedication of the Famous Five: Henrietta Muir Edwards, Nellie McClung, Louise McKinney, Emily Murphy and Irene Parlby.

These five were well-educated women working in Alberta to improve women's lives. They fought for a minimum wage for women, struggled to increase farm women's rights and battled to improve people's health, especially in frontier areas. All five women felt it was their responsibility to make changes in society so that everyone was treated fairly and equally.

Nellie McClung was well known across the country because she was one of the women battling to get western Canadian women the right to vote. In 1916 women in Alberta, Manitoba and Saskatchewan gained the right to vote in provincial elections. Other provinces and territories followed, and in 1918 women voted in federal elections for the first time.

It was because of Emily Murphy that the Famous Five came together. In 1916, on Emily's first day on the job as a magistrate (a type of judge), a lawyer told her that she had no right to be there. According to the British North America (BNA) Act, he said, a woman was not a person. Later, when women's groups were pressuring government to make Emily a senator, she faced the same argument — that a woman couldn't be appointed to Canada's Senate because she wasn't a person.

Emily got tired of being told that the law said she wasn't a person. She found out that she needed a group of five to challenge this ruling. So in 1927 the Famous Five joined together and sent a petition to the Supreme Court of Canada — the country's top law court — asking if the word "person" in the BNA Act included female persons. The Court debated for five weeks and decided that no, women were not included.

The Famous Five were shocked, but didn't give up their fight. They took the Persons Case, as it became known, to the Privy Council of England, Canada's highest court at that time. On October 18, 1929, the Council declared "that the exclusion of women from all public offices is a relic of days more barbarous than ours." Finally women were legally persons and so could hold any appointed or elected office.

The contributions the Famous Five made to society are recognized each year when the Governor General's Awards in Commemoration of the Persons Case are awarded to Canadians who work to improve women's equality.

When Women Got the Vote in Canada

- In federal elections, **1918**
- In provincial elections
  1916: Manitoba, Saskatchewan, Alberta
  1917: British Columbia, Ontario
  1918: Nova Scotia
  1919: New Brunswick, Yukon Territory
  1922: Prince Edward Island
  1925: Newfoundland and Labrador
  1940: Quebec
  1951: Northwest Territories (Nunavut was part of the Northwest Territories until 1999)

Henrietta Muir Edwards

Born: Dec. 18, 1849, at Montreal, PQ
Died: Nov. 10, 1931, at Fort Macleod, AB
Helped found the National Council
of Women and the Victorian Order
of Nurses

Louise McKinney

Born: Sept. 22, 1868, at Frankville, ON
Died: July 10, 1931, at Claresholm, AB
Was important in getting the vote for
women in Alberta and the first woman
elected to the Alberta legislature (also
the first woman in any legislature in the
British Commonwealth)

"THE PURPOSE OF A WOMAN'S
LIFE IS JUST THE SAME AS THE
PURPOSE OF A MAN'S LIFE: THAT
SHE MAY MAKE THE BEST POSSIBLE
CONTRIBUTION TO HER
GENERATION."

— *Louise McKinney*

Emily Murphy

Born: Mar. 14, 1868, at Cookstown, ON
Died: Oct. 27, 1933, at Edmonton, AB
Was the first woman magistrate
in Canada and in the British
Commonwealth, vice-president of the
National Council of Women of Canada
and a writer

"WHENEVER I DON'T KNOW
WHETHER TO FIGHT OR NOT, I
FIGHT."

— *Emily Murphy*

Nellie McClung

Born: Oct. 20, 1873, at Chatsworth, ON
Died: Sept. 1, 1951, at Victoria, BC
Led the fight to get Canadian women the
right to vote; was a member of the Alberta
legislature and a best-selling writer

"NEVER RETRACT, NEVER EXPLAIN,
NEVER APOLOGIZE — GET THINGS
DONE AND LET THEM HOWL."

— *Nellie McClung*

**When women gained the right
to vote, they could finally help
elect the politicians they wanted
and could have an effect on
government policy.**

Irene Parlby

Born: Jan. 9, 1868, at London, England
Died: July 12, 1965, at Red Deer, AB
Was the first woman to become a
member of the Cabinet (advisers to the
premier) in Alberta, the second woman
Cabinet member in the British
Commonwealth and president of the
United Farm Women of Alberta

EXPLORATION

First Nations people were Canada's earliest explorers. They travelled across Canada using their inventions — canoes, toboggans, snowshoes and more. There are no written records of their journeys, so there's no way to know for certain where they went.

When Europeans came to Canada, they wrote about the country's amazing size, rushing rivers, dense forests and bitter winters. These adventurers had never seen anything like Canada, and it would take all the courage and determination they had to explore it.

Jacques Cartier

Established the first permanent European settlement in Canada

Born: *between June 7 and Dec. 23, 1491, at St-Malo, France*

Died: *Sept. 1, 1557, at St-Malo, France*

The earliest Europeans who explored Canada were looking for a route to the riches of Asia. One of the first, Jacques Cartier, came from France in 1534 and explored the Gulf of St. Lawrence. Native people greeted him warmly — they didn't know that he'd already claimed their land for France.

When Jacques arrived back in France that September, he reported that the Native people were friendly and the country warmer than expected. So the French king sent Jacques back the next year. Jacques was a skilled navigator and easily made his way up the St. Lawrence River to the Native village of Stadacona (now Quebec City).

The chief, Donnacona, tried to convince Jacques not to go farther west, but the explorer was determined to see if the river was the route to Asia. He sailed to Hochelaga (at the site of what's now Montreal), where

he climbed the mountain (now called Mont Royal) for a better view. When Jacques saw the rapids upriver, he knew the river, the St. Lawrence, couldn't take him to Asia.

In Stadacona that winter, Jacques's men got sick with scurvy from a lack of vitamin C. The Native people made a cure from white cedar needles and bark, and most of the Europeans recovered. Jacques returned to France but came back to Canada in 1541. The Native people weren't as friendly — they'd found out that the French were claiming their land.

Jacques sailed home in 1542 with "gold" and "diamonds" that turned

out to be "fool's gold" and quartz. The French would show no interest in Canada for more than 50 years.

DID YOU KNOW

The name "Canada" comes from the Huron-Iroquois word *kanata*, meaning settlement. When one of Donnacona's sons showed Jacques the way to Canada, the son meant the route to his village — *kanata*. But Jacques thought the word described all the land.

John Cabot

First recorded European to discover and explore Canada

Born: 1449 or 1450, at Genoa, Italy

Died: 1498 or 1499, at sea, near Newfoundland

In 1497 John captained a British ship across the Atlantic Ocean. Unlike other explorers, such as

Most people know him as John Cabot, the English sailor, but he was born Giovanni Caboto in Italy. John was very eager to explore and find a shortcut to Asia. When he couldn't get anyone in Italy to fund his expedition, he headed to England in search of money and support.

Columbus, he stayed in the North Atlantic area.

On June 24, 1497, John reached land. On his return to England, he told of a "new founde land" — today Canada's easternmost province, Newfoundland and Labrador. John also reported that there were huge numbers of fish. This news would lead European fishers to Newfoundland's rich fishing banks.

John sailed again to Canada in May 1498. But he disappeared off the coast of Newfoundland, and no one knows what happened to him.

Samuel de Champlain

Founder of New France

Born: about 1570, at Brouage, France

Died: Dec. 25, 1635, at Quebec City, PQ

Samuel de Champlain first came to Canada in 1603. He wasn't an explorer then — his job was to record the story of the voyage and draw the maps. The next year, he mapped the Acadia area of what is now Nova Scotia, looking for a good place for a settlement. During this time, he set up the Order of Good Cheer to take the minds of his fellow Frenchmen off the harsh conditions. This was the first club started by Europeans in North America.

In 1608 Samuel headed to the Native village of Stadacona to establish a French settlement. He called it Quebec, which comes from an Algonquian word meaning "where the river narrows." The next year,

while exploring, Samuel and a group of Huron allies got into a battle with some Iroquois warriors. Samuel shot an Iroquois chief, and from then on the Iroquois considered the French their enemies.

Samuel dreamed that the new colony would be the centre of a new French world in which French and Native people were united. He set up trading networks throughout the area to ensure the survival of the colony, called New France. But

Samuel never lost sight of France's goal — finding a passage through Canada to Asia.

When the English gained control of New France from 1629 to 1632, Samuel was taken prisoner to England, then finally returned to France. He sailed back to Quebec in 1633 to lead the colony as its first governor.

DID YOU KNOW

Samuel de Champlain wanted to call the Quebec settlement Ludovica, which means, "If it pleases God and the King."

Martin Frobisher

Arctic explorer

Born: 1535 or 1539, near Wakefield, England

Died: Nov. 24, 1594, at Plymouth, England

Greed brought explorer Martin Frobisher to Canada. He was looking for an Arctic route to the riches of Asia — the Northwest Passage. Martin was an English privateer (a type of pirate) who'd been given permission by the queen of England to steal from enemy ships. Between 1576 and 1578, he made three trips to Canada's North looking for the Northwest Passage and discovered a bay that is now named after him — Frobisher Bay.

Martin brought boatloads of "gold" back to England, but it all turned out to be worthless "fool's gold." He also found a "unicorn horn" — probably the tusk from a narwhal. Thanks to Martin's voyages, more and more explorers were drawn to Canada's Arctic in search of treasure and the Northwest Passage.

Henry Hudson

First European explorer to sail into Hudson Bay

Born: around 1570, probably in Hertfordshire, England

Died: 1611, at Hudson Bay

Finding the Northwest Passage — a route through the icy waters of Canada's Arctic to Asia — was an obsession for English sailor Henry Hudson. He was a good sailor and navigator, but his relentless search would eventually kill him.

Henry first tried to find a passage through the Arctic islands in 1607 and then again in 1608. Both times he was stopped by ice floes. In 1609 he tried yet again, this time farther south, exploring what is now the east coast of the United States. The Hudson River in New York state is named after him.

In 1610 Henry was back trying a northern route. He headed through the rough water north of what's now Labrador and down into the bay that came to be named after him. Henry sailed on, thinking he had found the Northwest Passage. But he hadn't. Instead he had sailed into James Bay, where his ship became stuck in the ice. Henry and his men had to spend the winter on their icebound ship. They were cold and hungry, and many also became sick.

Henry was strong and brave, but he wasn't good at managing his crew. When he announced the next spring that they'd be continuing the search for the Northwest Passage, the men mutinied. Henry, his son and seven others were forced into a small boat and set adrift. They were never seen again.

Many of the crew didn't make it home to England. Those who did were tried for murder. However, these men had valuable knowledge about this new area of Canada. Their knowledge would be lost if they were found guilty and executed, so they were allowed to live.

Alexander Mackenzie

First European to travel overland across Canada

Born: *1764, at Stornoway, Scotland*

Died: *Mar. 12, 1820, near Dunkeld, Scotland*

Finding a route across Canada to the Pacific Ocean was fur trader Alexander Mackenzie's dream. He tried first in 1789, when he followed a large river west from Lake Athabaska, on the border between Alberta and Saskatchewan.

Unfortunately for Alexander, the river turned north. When he and his Native guides reached the Arctic Ocean and saw ice floes in the water, he knew they hadn't reached the Western Sea, as the Pacific was called then. Alexander named the waterway River Disappointment, but it was later named the Mackenzie River after him.

Determined to try again, Alexander prepared by learning more about mapmaking and the stars, to improve his navigation skills. Then in 1792 he set out to find the Pacific Ocean with six voyageurs (fur traders and adventurers who travelled across Canada in canoes), two Native guides and a dog.

Thanks to his determination and skills — which he was quite proud of — the group moved safely and incredibly quickly across the rugged Rocky Mountains, then down wild rivers to the Pacific. On July 22, 1793, Alexander became the first European to cross North America and find a pass through the Rockies.

DID YOU KNOW

The dog that travelled with Alexander Mackenzie didn't ride in the canoe. The dog — it was just known as "Our Dog" — swam beside the canoe or ran along the riverbank. When the men had to climb through mountains, Our Dog climbed with them.

David Thompson

Canada's first geographer

Born: *Apr. 30, 1770, at London, England*

Died: *Feb. 10, 1857, at Longueuil, PQ*

While recovering from a broken leg in 1790, David Thompson spent his time in Cumberland House (in what's now Saskatchewan) studying surveying and navigation by the stars. His goal? To map western Canada.

By 1793 David had mapped most of northern Manitoba and Saskatchewan for the Hudson's Bay Company. Then he switched to the North West Company because he felt they were more adventurous. He travelled more than 90 000 km (56 000 mi.) across Canada, often with his children — he'd eventually have 13 — and his wife.

David's final map recorded more than one-third of the area of Canada and covered a whole wall. This very precise map was still in use in the early 1900s.

John Franklin

An interest in maps and weather led English adventurer John Franklin to explore Canada's North. During an expedition in 1819–1822, he mapped 2900 km (1800 mi.) of Arctic coastline. Then he and his crew ran out of food and had to eat the leather parts of their clothes. Ten men died of cold and hunger. When John returned to England, he was greeted as a hero for enduring the terrible conditions.

John's next trip in 1825 was much more successful. He mapped 1500 km (930 mi.) of coastline and collected data on rocks, weather and 663 plants.

By 1845, although he hadn't been to the Arctic for 20 years, John was still considered by many to be the best man to lead an expedition there. He and his crew sailed in ships with iron-covered bows to help them push through the ice. Despite their precautions, they became stuck near King William Island in the summer of 1846.

For almost two years, they were icebound — even in summer they couldn't escape. John and his whole crew disappeared and were never seen again.

It took an 11-year search to solve the mystery of what happened to the Franklin expedition. No one knows how the men spent their last days, but they were probably poisoned by lead in the cans containing their food.

DID YOU KNOW

On John Franklin's last journey, his ship was stocked with clothing, tobacco, rum, 8000 tins of food and more than 2000 books.

Simon Fraser

Daring and brave, Simon Fraser is famous for exploring the interior of what is now British Columbia. He set up forts for the North West Company there and in Alberta.

In 1808 he tried to find a route that the company's fur traders could take to the Pacific Ocean. He and 20

men canoed down a river that Simon thought was the Columbia. It turned out to be 835 km (520 mi.) of rough water and almost impossible portages — one of Canada's greatest explorations. "We had to pass where no human being should venture," wrote Simon.

When Simon got to the end of the river, he realized that it wasn't the Columbia, and that it was too rough to use as a trade route. Although he couldn't know it then, the Fraser River — as it was later named — proved to be an important route through the Rockies for the railways and highways that were built along its banks.

Roberta Bondar

First Canadian woman in space

Born: *Dec. 4, 1945, at Sault Ste. Marie, ON*

For Roberta Bondar, the dream of flying through space began when she looked up at the stars as a young girl. In school she studied science and became a neurologist (a doctor who studies the brain). Her determination and high energy helped her succeed. Roberta kept alive her desire to fly by becoming a pilot — she could fly a plane before she could drive a car.

When Canada advertised for astronauts, thousands of people applied. Roberta was proud to be one of the first six Canadians chosen, along with Marc Garneau, below. Learning to be an astronaut takes time and hard work. Roberta began her training in 1984, but it wasn't until January 1992 that she became the first Canadian woman in space, aboard the space shuttle *Discovery*.

During her eight days on the shuttle, Roberta performed experiments in the spacelab. Many people later asked her what it was like being a woman astronaut, but being a *Canadian* astronaut was much more important to Roberta. "How many Canadians do you think I'm carrying on my shoulder?" she asked. "But they don't weigh anything in space …"

Marc Garneau

First Canadian in space

Born: *Feb. 23, 1949, at Quebec City, PQ*

Marc Garneau never dreamed of being an astronaut because he thought Canadians would never have the chance to explore space. That changed in 1983 when he saw an advertisement saying Canada was looking for astronauts. Marc was one of the lucky six picked from more than 4000 applicants. After a few months of training, his career was launched.

"THERE WAS A LOT OF PRESSURE BECAUSE IT WAS THE FIRST TIME, IT WAS BRAND NEW FOR CANADA … "

— *Marc Garneau*

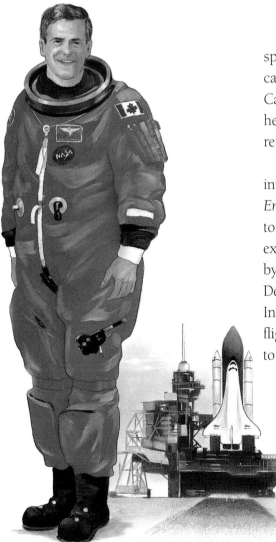

In October 1984, aboard the space shuttle *Challenger*, this quiet, careful engineer became the first Canadian in space. Marc made sure he had a hockey puck with him to represent his home country.

In May 1996, Marc rocketed into space again, this time on the *Endeavour*. He used the Canadarm to retrieve a satellite and carried out experiments, including two designed by Canadian kids. He returned in December 2000 to help build the International Space Station. With this flight, Marc became the first Canadian to fly three missions in space.

SCIENCE & TECHNOLOGY

Canadian scientists, doctors and inventors have left their mark on the world. Some have transformed how we communicate, changed how we get around and improved our health. Others have surveyed our country, lit up the world and even altered the way we tell time.

You may not have heard of some of the Canadians described here, while others are famous around the world. They're all great Canadians who found unique ways to change the world of science and technology. Millions of people have benefited from their work.

Frederick Banting & Charles Best

Discoverers of insulin

Frederick Banting

Born: Nov. 14, 1891, at Alliston, ON

Died: Feb. 21, 1941, near Musgrave Harbour, NF

Charles Best

Born: Feb. 27, 1899, at West Pembroke, ME, U.S.

Died: Mar. 31, 1978, at Toronto, ON

In 1921 Charles Best had just finished his degree in biochemistry and physiology (sciences that study how living organisms work) when his boss at the University of Toronto, Professor John Macleod, gave him the chance to work on experiments with Frederick Banting. Charles leaped at the chance — Frederick was trying to find a treatment for diabetes, a killer disease. Little did Charles know that this work would make him famous in the world of medicine years before he became a doctor.

Doctors knew that diabetes was caused by the lack of a hormone called insulin. But they couldn't figure out how to supply needed insulin to patients. Frederick had an idea, and he was determined to make it work.

He and Charles tried injecting diabetic dogs with an insulin solution. James Collip, the other key team member, purified the insulin they used.

When the dogs were treated with the insulin, they improved. In 1922 insulin was successfully tested on a human. This was a major medical breakthrough, and the team won many awards, including a Nobel Prize (page 56). While insulin isn't a cure, it helps control diabetes and has saved the lives of millions of people.

DID YOU KNOW

Charles had to toss a coin with a classmate to decide who would start working with Frederick. Luckily for Charles, he won the toss!

Sandford Fleming

Inventor of Standard Time

Born: Jan. 7, 1827, at Kirkcaldy, Scotland

Died: July 22, 1915, at Halifax, NS

In 1863 Sandford Fleming was made chief surveyor of the railway between Quebec City and Saint John, New Brunswick. He used what he knew about the railways and the geography of the area to figure out the best route for the tracks.

When the first transcontinental railway was planned between Montreal and the Pacific Ocean in 1871, Sandford was the engineer in charge, this time surveying the prairies and the Rocky Mountains. His energy, intelligence and desire to unite Canada made him perfect for the job.

But when the railway began running across Canada, there were problems timing the trains. Back then, everyone told time by the sun. Noon occurred when the sun was directly overhead. So noon in one town wasn't necessarily noon in another town. In fact, at one point there were 144 "official" local times in North America.

The different local times caused railway accidents, and many passengers had to carry several watches. So Sandford proposed Standard Time, a system that would divide the world into just 24 time zones.

The idea was so revolutionary that at first it was rejected. But Sandford was committed and kept pushing for it. Because of his efforts, Standard Time came into use around the world on January 1, 1885. The railways were especially grateful.

DID YOU KNOW

In 1851 Sandford Fleming designed Canada's first postage stamp, the Threepenny Beaver. Today the stamp in good condition is worth more than $15 000.

William Logan

First director of the Geological Survey of Canada

Born: Apr. 20, 1798, at Montreal, PQ

Died: June 22, 1875, at Castle Malgwyn, Cilgerran, South Wales

In his mid-thirties, while working in his uncle's coal mine in Wales, William Logan became interested in geology (the study of rocks). The geology maps of the time weren't detailed enough for him, so he made his own. These maps included cross-sections of Earth's

layers for the first time. In 1840, using what he knew about rocks, William solved the mystery of how coal is formed — he figured out that it's compressed ancient plant material.

William returned to Canada from Wales and founded the Geological Survey of Canada in 1842. His goal was to map the rock features of the area that's now Ontario and Quebec for the first time. The maps helped launch mining in Canada, which became one of the most important industries in the country.

Mount Logan, Canada's highest mountain, is named after William.

Alexander Graham Bell

Inventor of the telephone

Born: *Mar. 3, 1847, at Edinburgh, Scotland*

Died: *Aug. 2, 1922, at Baddeck, NS*

Sound and speech were always on Alexander Graham Bell's mind. His mother was deaf, and his father taught people how to speak clearly. By 1870 both of his brothers had died of lung disease, so his parents decided to move to where the air was clean — Canada. In 1871 "Aleck" began teaching at a school for the deaf in Boston, Massachusetts. He was a patient and inventive teacher.

At night, Aleck experimented with sound. He wanted to improve the telegraph, an instrument that sent and received electric pulses over wires. In 1874 he had a breakthrough while visiting his parents in Brantford, Ontario. Aleck realized that with a few changes to the telegraph, he could

pick up all the sounds of the human voice. The voice moved thin metal disks, and these disks could change electric currents, allowing voices to be sent and received over wires.

Knowing how to do something and actually doing it are very different things, Aleck found. Almost two years later, on March 10, 1876, Aleck was in one room tinkering with a transmitter, while his assistant, Thomas Watson, had a receiver connected by wire in another room. When Aleck accidentally spilled some acid, he shouted into his transmitter, "Mr. Watson — Come here — I want to see you!"

Thomas came running into the room — he'd heard Aleck's voice over the receiver. The telephone was born. In a few months, Aleck also figured out how to send telephone messages long distance, between two cities.

Aleck went on to invent many things, from iceberg detectors to

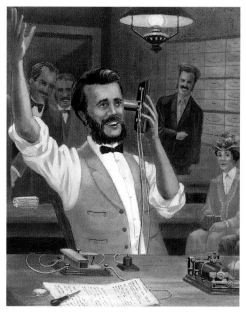

airplanes that set flight records. But he often said he preferred to be known as someone who had helped deaf people communicate.

> "AN INVENTOR CAN NO MORE HELP INVENTING THAN HE CAN HELP THINKING OR BREATHING."
>
> — *Alexander Graham Bell*

Reginald Fessenden

Inventor who made the first radio voice broadcast

Born: *Oct. 6, 1866, at Milton-Est, PQ*

Died: *July 22, 1932, at Hamilton, Bermuda*

When Reginald Fessenden was just 10 years old, he watched Alexander Graham Bell demonstrate the telephone by transmitting voices over wires between Brantford and Paris, Ontario. Reginald began to dream of broadcasting voices *without* wires.

Few people thought wireless broadcasting of voices and music was possible. When Reginald asked

Thomas Edison what he thought about the likelihood, the great inventor said, "Fezzie, what do you say are man's chances of jumping over the moon? I think one is as likely as the other." But on Christmas Eve 1906, Reginald used radio waves to transmit his voice — and Christmas music — without wires. It was the first radio broadcast ever.

During his lifetime, Reginald created more than 500 inventions. He also built Niagara Falls's first power-generating station.

Armand Bombardier

Inventor of the snowmobile

Born: Apr. 16, 1907, at Valcourt, PQ

Died: Feb. 18, 1964, at Sherbrooke, PQ

When Armand Bombardier was a child, driving through snow in his hometown of Valcourt, Quebec, was tough. Since Armand loved working on machines and was good at it, he and his brother Léopold decided to create a vehicle to carry people *over* the snow. In 1922, when Armand was just 15, the brothers attached a car motor and an airplane propeller to a sleigh. The boys amazed the neighbours with their snow machine.

Trained as a mechanic, Armand opened a garage in 1926 and spent his spare time experimenting with snow vehicles. He developed a machine with steerable skis and a set of caterpillar tracks, and, in 1937, produced a vehicle that could carry seven people over snow.

Armand was also a clever and creative business man, and he dreamed of inventing a smaller machine for one or two people. In 1959 he created the Ski-Doo snowmobile. It changed how people got around in winter, especially in the Arctic, and created a whole new winter sport.

DID YOU KNOW

The company Armand Bombardier founded is the world's largest railway equipment manufacturer and the third-biggest maker of aircraft.

Abraham Gesner

Inventor of kerosene

Born: May 2, 1797, near Cornwallis, NS

Died: Apr. 29, 1864, at Halifax, NS

As a boy, Abraham Gesner collected rocks and fossils. He later became a doctor, but between house calls he would pick up rock specimens. In 1842 he opened his own museum — the first museum in Canada — and displayed his collection.

Smart and creative, Abraham learned more about rocks and also became interested in oil and coal, which are found in rock. Around 1846 he saw the need for a lamp oil that was bright and clear, not smelly and smoky like the whale oil used at the time. By 1853 Abraham had developed a type of coal oil that he called "kerosene," from the Greek words for wax and oil. Soon it was lighting homes across North America, and today's jet fuel is based on it.

Leonora Howard King

First Canadian doctor in China

Born: *Mar. 17, 1851, at Farmersville (now Athens), ON*

Died: *June 30, 1925, at Tientsin (now Tianjin), China*

Her desire to be a doctor took Leonora Howard King away from Canada. In the 1870s, Canadian medical schools wouldn't teach women. Smart and determined, Leonora headed to the United States instead, and graduated with honours in 1876. The new doctor sailed to China the next year, looking for adventure and a chance to spread Christianity.

In China, Leonora treated both royalty and poor people, especially women and children, often without pay. For her work, she was made a mandarin (similar to a knight). She was the first North American woman to earn such a rare honour from China. But for Leonora, helping people was much more important.

Norman Bethune

Surgeon and inventor

Born: *Mar. 3, 1890, at Gravenhurst, ON*

Died: *Nov. 12, 1939, at Huang Shiko, China*

When Henry Norman Bethune was just eight, he stuck on his bedroom door the nameplate that had belonged to his surgeon grandfather. It seems he was already on his way to a medical career.

Norman served in Europe during World War I, carrying wounded men on stretchers. He was shipped back to Canada when he, too, was badly wounded. While recovering, he got his medical degree and began treating patients. But in 1926 Norman became ill with tuberculosis (a lung disease). He was sure he was going to die from it — as many people did — until he read about a possible surgical treatment for the disease. Norman arranged to try it, and it cured him, so he learned how to perform the surgery himself.

Norman became well known as a surgeon specializing in diseases of the chest, heart and lungs. The shears he invented for cutting ribs were so well designed that they're still used today.

When civil war in Spain broke out in 1936, Norman was asked to head a medical team there. While treating wounded patients, he invented a mobile blood bank that could be wheeled onto the battlefield. He performed blood transfusions in the midst of battle and saved many lives.

Norman is probably best known for the time he spent in China — from 1938 until his death — treating Chinese soldiers during a war with Japan and training many Chinese people as doctors. There he invented a mobile medical unit equipped with basic life-saving supplies. Norman's accomplishments have saved lives all over the world.

DID YOU KNOW

Norman Bethune is such a hero in China that a hospital, museum, pavilion and statue have been erected next to his tomb there.

William Osler

Doctor, educator, writer

Born: *July 12, 1849, at Bond Head, ON*

Died: *Dec. 29, 1919, at Oxford, England*

William Osler transformed the way medicine is taught, not only in Canada but around the world. Up to the late 1800s, medical students spent most of their time in lecture halls or labs and rarely saw sick people. William thought that student doctors should learn from patients, so he increased the hours of patient-student contact.

William also gave lessons at the bedsides of sick people because he knew this was an effective way of training students. His students learned from him how important it is to listen very carefully to the patient when making a diagnosis.

Besides being an excellent teacher, William was also an expert in diagnosing diseases of the heart, lungs and blood. Friendly and outgoing, he knew how to inspire his patients with hope. He had a good sense of humour and liked to play practical jokes on friends.

In 1892 William wrote a medical textbook that was used for more than 40 years. As well, he helped create the system of post-graduate training for doctors that's still followed today. By the end of the 1800s, William was one of the best-known doctors in the world.

"WE ARE HERE TO ADD WHAT WE CAN TO LIFE, NOT TO GET WHAT WE CAN FROM IT."

— *William Osler*

Emily Stowe

Suffragist and first Canadian woman to work as a doctor

Born: *May 1, 1831, at Norwich, ON*

Died: *Apr. 30, 1903, at Toronto, ON*

Well educated and interested in herbal medicine, Emily Stowe wanted to become a doctor. But she was a woman, and women weren't allowed to study medicine in Canada in the 1860s. Emily believed strongly that men and women are equal, so she went to New York to study medicine.

Even with her American medical licence, Emily wasn't allowed to practise medicine in Canada. She decided to do it anyway, despite fines and threats. Finally, in 1880, she was granted a Canadian licence. She wasn't the first woman to get a licence in Canada — her friend Jenny

Trout had been given hers in 1875 — but Emily was instrumental in changing the rules to allow women to work as doctors. As a suffragist she also campaigned for women's right to vote.

DID YOU KNOW

Before Emily Stowe became a doctor, she became Canada's first woman school principal, in 1852.

BUSINESS

Canada's great natural resources and its vast geography have shaped Canadian business. Some businesses have harvested resources, such as timber and minerals. Some have manufactured resources into new products. And others have made a business of transporting materials and machinery.

But business is more than just making money. Top business people see a need and fill it, or create something new and help it grow. Their innovations provide jobs for Canadians. And business people who succeed often go on to make a special contribution to society, either by helping people in need or by supporting Canadian culture.

Alphonse Desjardins

Founder of the caisse populaire
(credit union)

Born: Nov. 5, 1854, at Lévis, PQ

Died: Oct. 31, 1920, at Lévis, PQ

In 1897 a member of Parliament stood up in the House of Commons in Ottawa and talked about a family forced to pay back $5000 for a $150 loan. When Alphonse Desjardins heard this, he was horrified. He came from a poor family and knew how difficult it was for workers to borrow money at a reasonable rate. Alphonse also saw how many farmers were being forced off their farms for lack of money and were leaving Canada for the United States. He decided to change things.

Alphonse read about different types of banks around the world and discussed his ideas with experts. On December 6, 1900, he opened North America's first *caisse populaire*, or people's bank. Also known as a credit union, a *caisse populaire* is a kind of co-op that lends money to its members at low interest rates.

Sometimes the loans were for less than $100 — too small for most banks — but the loans made a difference to the person's life.

By the time Alphonse died 20 years later, he had set up 206 *caisses populaires* in Quebec, Ontario and the U.S. He became a world-famous authority on co-operative financial institutions. Today there are more than 1200 *caisses populaires* in Canada and the U.S., and the concept has spread around the world. People in Quebec are reminded of Alphonse's compassion and caring by the hundreds of awards and scholarships named after him.

DID YOU KNOW

Alphonse Desjardins thought it was really important that kids learn to save, so he promoted the idea of a student saving program called *caisse scolaire*.

Samuel Cunard

Shipping innovator

Born: Nov. 21, 1787, at Halifax, NS

Died: Apr. 28, 1865, at London, England

In the 1830s, sailing ships that travelled between Canada and England were at the mercy of the wind. As a result, their sailing times were unpredictable. Businessman Samuel Cunard decided to change that. In 1833 his ship the *Royal William* travelled from Canada to England, making it the first ship to cross the Atlantic Ocean using its own power — steam. Soon steamships routinely crossed the Atlantic.

Samuel was a skilled business-man. In 1840 he started the first regular mail service between Liverpool, England, and Halifax, Nova Scotia. He was also daring, sending his ships across the North Atlantic in winter, when no other ship owner would.

Ocean transportation was transformed by Samuel. He thought of his shipping line as an "ocean railway," with ships coming and going on schedule. His ships were the first to be lit by electricity and use wireless communication. His passenger ships, such as the *Queen Elizabeth*, were the best of their time. Cunard Lines is one of the oldest shipping lines still sailing.

DID YOU KNOW

Samuel Cunard started the system of sailing with green lights to starboard (the right side of the ship) and red to port (left), which all sailors now use.

Timothy Eaton

Sales innovator

Born: 1834, near Ballymena, Ireland

Died: Jan. 31, 1907, at Toronto, ON

Timothy Eaton changed the way Canadians shop. In 1869 he opened a store in Toronto based on three promises: fixed prices, cash only, and satisfaction guaranteed or money refunded.

What a difference! Up to then, shoppers and store owners would haggle over dollars and cents, but "fixed prices" meant everyone knew the cost. "Cash only" put an end to bartering for goods and gave the shop owner more money to pay the bills. And "satisfaction guaranteed or money refunded" gave the buyer peace of mind — if the goods were

faulty, the store promised to take them back.

Timothy wanted to sell to more people, including those living outside of Toronto. So in 1884 he put out a

mail-order catalogue. It became known as the "Farmer's Bible." People shopped from the Eaton's catalogue — and also used it for hockey shin pads, building insulation and toilet paper!

Sam McLaughlin

President of Canada's first car company

Born: Sept. 8, 1871, at Enniskillen, ON

Died: Jan. 6, 1972, at Oshawa, ON

At 16, Robert Samuel McLaughlin started working in his father's carriage factory for $3.00 per week — minus $2.50 that his father deducted for room and meals. Despite the low pay, Sam soon designed more than 140 models of carriages and sleighs. He was especially good with fabric and upholstery.

DID YOU KNOW

The McLaughlin Foundation, which Sam started, gave away almost $200 million to help Canadians.

Sam got his first ride in an automobile in 1904. It had no doors, top or windows, and passengers got soaked in the rain. So the car owner asked Sam to design something to help keep them dry. Sam made a cover for the car and, as a thank you, the owner let him drive it. Travel and speed had always fascinated Sam, and he was soon hooked on cars.

In 1907, in Oshawa, Ontario, Sam set up the McLaughlin Motor Car Company, with himself as president. This was the first major car manufacturer in Canada — the company created the first car assembled in Canada. Sam sold his company to the General Motors Company in 1918 but stayed on as president.

Now a rich man, Sam believed in sharing his wealth. One of his main interests was Canadians' health, so he supported medical research. He also helped many arts, education and community groups.

Hart Massey

Farm machinery manufacturer

Born: Apr. 29, 1823, at Haldimand Township, ON

Died: Feb. 20, 1896, at Toronto, ON

Ontario's Massey family were skilled business people who understood the importance of producing up-to-date machinery. But Hart Massey made the Massey Manufacturing Company especially successful by merging it with other companies. He used bold advertising and sales techniques and was always looking for ways to improve the company's products.

Under his leadership in the 1780s, the company became the first in North America to export farm machinery to countries around the world.

Hart gave generously to many charities and built Massey Hall in Toronto in 1894. His grandson Raymond was a famous actor. Grandson Vincent was Canada's first Canadian-born Governor General.

DID YOU KNOW

The Massey Manufacturing Company transformed farming in Canada. Production soared, thanks to new machines that made farmers' work easier.

Donald Smith

Fur trader, politician and railway supporter

Born: *Aug. 6, 1820, at Forres, Scotland*

Died: *Jan. 21, 1914, at London, England*

Clever and kind, Donald Smith moved up through the Hudson's Bay Company (HBC) of fur traders — from the very junior position of apprentice clerk in 1838 to governor by 1889.

As he worked with the HBC, Donald came to know a lot about the prairies. So in 1869 the Canadian government sent him to the Red River Settlement, in today's Manitoba, to negotiate with Louis Riel (page 44). Louis was angry because the HBC was transferring the rights for a large area of land to Canada. He and his Métis followers (people of First Nations and European descent) claimed some of the land. Donald negotiated with Louis and helped end the dispute (called the Red River Rebellion). Soon Donald became a member of Manitoba's and Canada's governments.

Donald helped create the Canadian Pacific Railway Company in 1880 to build a rail line across the country. A number of times during construction money almost ran out, so Donald invested his own money. As a thank-you, he was invited to drive the last spike when the railway was finished in 1885 (right). He was also made 1st Baron Strathcona and Mount Royal.

In 1890 Donald created the Strathcona Horse — 600 Canadian riders led by Sam Steele (page 9) — to fight for Britain in the South African (Boer) war. Called "Lord Strathcona's Horse (Royal Canadians)" since 1940, the unit has been one of Canada's most famous regiments. Donald also helped fund Montreal's Royal Victoria Hospital.

DID YOU KNOW

Donald Smith tried to protect prairie bison and at one point owned the last free-roaming herd.

William Van Horne

Builder of Canada's transcontinental railway

Born: *Feb. 3, 1843, at Chelsea, IL, U.S.*

Died: *Sept. 11, 1915, at Montreal, PQ*

Work on the Canadian Pacific Railway (CPR) — Canada's transcontinental railway line — started in 1875. It was supposed to be finished by 1880, but by 1881, it was clear that the job was tougher than anyone had thought. The CPR decided it needed someone who really knew railways, so they hired William Van Horne. He'd started working around railways when he was 14, and he loved and understood the business.

William divided the route across the country into sections and had teams of workers start in different places. The workers had to cross deep gorges, treacherous swamps, the rugged Rocky Mountains and other tough terrain, but by 1885 the job was done. William became president of the CPR in 1888 and worked hard to make the company grow. When William died, the CPR halted all trains for a whole day.

Elizabeth Arden

Cosmetics innovator

Born: *Dec. 31, 1878, at Woodbridge, ON*

Died: *Oct. 19, 1966, at New York City, NY, U.S.*

Named Florence Nightingale Graham at birth, Elizabeth Arden seemed destined to become a nurse. But when she tried nursing, the young Florence soon found she was too squeamish for the job. Still, her work with burn victims taught her how much appearance and self-esteem are linked, and she dreamed of creating beauty products.

Florence began making skin creams in her kitchen. Some of them smelled like rotten eggs, but she didn't give up. In 1910 she opened her own beauty salon in New York and gave herself a new name —

Elizabeth Arden. Women flocked to the salon. Until then, makeup was usually worn only on stage, but by the 1920s Elizabeth helped make it available to everyone. A good trend spotter, she was continually creating new products. She introduced eye makeup to North America, and once made a skin cream out of a product developed for her racehorses. When Elizabeth found that the cream soothed the grooms' hands, she began to sell it to her customers.

Elizabeth was also one of the first to make exercise records and to bring yoga exercises into her salons. She became a multi-millionaire, and today her products are sold around the world.

"GO OUT AND MAKE YOUR MARK."

— *Elizabeth Arden*

Max Aitken

Businessman, politician, writer, newspaper publisher

Born: *May 25, 1879, at Maple, ON*

Died: *June 9, 1964, at Mickleham, England*

By the time he was 29, William Maxwell "Max" Aitken had made his first million. He did it by selling bonds (investments) in Canadian companies.

In 1910 Max moved to England where he became a politician. When World War I broke out four years later, he worked in Europe, sending reports on Canadian troops back to Canada. For his work in the war and in politics, Max was named 1st Baron Beaverbrook in 1917. The name "Beaverbrook" comes from a stream near his Canadian home.

But things in politics happened too slowly for Max. He decided instead to create a chain of British newspapers. By 1960 he owned the largest-selling British newspaper and had become extremely wealthy.

DID YOU KNOW

For many years, shows in movie theatres began with a short film about events in the news. Max Aitken introduced this feature.

Roy Thomson

Newspaper publisher

Born: June 5, 1894, at Toronto, ON

Died: Aug. 4, 1976, at London, England

Roy Thomson was having a tough time selling radios around North Bay, Ontario, in 1931. With no radio stations in the area, the reception quality was poor. So Roy decided to set up his own radio station. Soon radio sales soared, and he started more stations.

Downstairs in the building of the Timmins, Ontario, radio station, Roy found a printing press from an old newspaper. He bought it to start his own newspaper. Roy continued to buy more radio stations — and newspapers. In the 1950s, he branched out into other countries, buying newspapers, magazines and television stations.

Because of Roy's success running several British newspapers, the British government named him Baron Thomson of Fleet. Roy Thomson Hall in Toronto, the city's largest concert hall, is named after him.

"I THINK THAT A LOT OF OWNERS OF NEWSPAPERS GET BEDAZZLED WITH THE IMPORTANCE WHICH THEY THINK THEY HAVE … WHEREAS I AM COLD-BLOODEDLY A BUSINESSMAN."

— *Roy Thomson*

Floyd Chalmers

Supporter of arts and culture

Born: Sept. 14, 1898, at Chicago, IL, U.S.

Died: Apr. 26, 1993, at Toronto, ON

Successful businessman Floyd Chalmers once said that "he could see no point in being a rich man" and so gave away millions of dollars to arts and education organizations.

Floyd began his career as a newspaper reporter when he was just 17. He moved up through the newspaper and magazine business, becoming president of one of Canada's largest magazine publishers in 1950.

Long before that, he and his wife began giving away their money. Their projects included forming the Canadian Opera Company and building a theatre for the Stratford Festival in Stratford, Ontario. The Chalmers Program continues to help many artists today.

DID YOU KNOW

Floyd Chalmers was especially interested in helping young artists and supporting new arts projects.

THE ARTS

Canadian actors, musicians, painters and writers are known around the world. They write best-selling books and record CDs that sell millions, influencing what the world reads, listens to, watches and thinks.

Canadian artists and performers remind us who we are and why we love Canada. They also give other countries a glimpse of the colourful mosaic of people that make up this amazing land and reveal what's important to us.

Lucy Maud Montgomery

Children's writer

Born: Nov. 30, 1874, at Clifton (now New London), PE

Died: Apr. 24, 1942, at Toronto, ON

Anne of Green Gables, Emily of New Moon, Pat of Silver Bush — these are just a few of the wonderful children's books that sprang from the pen of Lucy Maud Montgomery. She wrote 24 books, 530 short stories and more than 500 poems during her lifetime. In the process, she introduced her beloved Prince Edward Island and Canada to the world.

Maud — she hated being called Lucy — had a difficult childhood. Her mother died before she was two, and she was left with her mother's strict parents while her father headed to Saskatchewan for work. Maud felt lonely and unloved, which was why she would later feel so comfortable writing about orphans.

Maud became a schoolteacher, but spent her spare time writing short stories and poems. Later she earned a living from these, but she longed to write a book. That seemed like an impossible dream, until Maud got an idea for a wonderful character — a red-haired orphan named Anne. It took Maud months to write Anne's story, fitting it in between her other writing and chores.

Maud proudly sent off her manuscript to a publisher. But it quickly came back — rejected. That happened four more times! Maud was very discouraged and put the story aside for a few months. Then she decided to send it out one last time. Finally Maud's manuscript was accepted, and on June 20, 1908, Maud opened the package that held her first book, *Anne of Green Gables*.

Today Maud's books are read around the world. *Anne of Green Gables* has been published in more than 20 languages and has sold tens of millions of copies.

"I BELIEVED IN MYSELF AND I STRUGGLED ON ALONE, IN SECRECY AND SILENCE. I NEVER TOLD MY AMBITIONS AND EFFORTS AND FAILURES TO ANY ONE."

— *Lucy Maud Montgomery*

Oscar Peterson

Jazz pianist

Born: Aug. 15, 1925, at Montreal, PQ

As a teenager in Montreal, Oscar Peterson found that playing piano was a great way to attract girls. He won a national music contest when he was just 14 and soon was playing jazz piano on radio shows broadcast across the country.

By 1948 Oscar's speedy fingers and musical sense had him playing with the best jazz musicians. He formed the Oscar Peterson Trio, and it soon became known as the hardest-working group in jazz. One year the trio recorded 11 albums. Despite his success, Oscar had to deal with prejudice because of his skin colour.

In a career of more than 50 years, Oscar has recorded lots of top-selling albums, gained millions of fans and become a jazz composer. He has received many awards for his music, including the Praemium Imperiale Award (1999), an important international prize for artists.

Glenn Gould

Classical pianist

Born: Sept. 25, 1932, at Toronto, ON

Died: Oct. 4, 1982, at Toronto, ON

At age three, Glenn Gould could already read music. He began to compose when he was just five. By 14 he was performing as a solo pianist with the Toronto Symphony Orchestra, and within a few years he was one of Canada's most important musicians.

Glenn performed all over the world, and his performances were legendary. He sat in a low, rickety-looking chair, humming or singing along (you can hear him on some of his recordings) and conducting himself. People made such a fuss over these unusual habits that in 1964 Glenn stopped performing in public. He even came to be known as a bit of a hermit.

But Glenn continued to record music — especially by composer J.S. Bach. In all he made more than 60 recordings, cutting and splicing until he had the most perfect version he could make. Glenn appeared in several films and television shows. He also created radio programs, including one about his favourite part of Canada, the Far North.

Mary Pickford

Actor

Born: *Apr. 9, 1892, at Toronto, ON*

Died: *May 25, 1979, at Santa Monica, CA, U.S.*

Gladys Louise Smith was a child actor in Toronto theatre during the early 1900s. Although she was a good actor, she didn't make much money. So her mother moved the family to New York, hoping her daughter might strike it rich.

Gladys's career took off. Her mother convinced her to try out for the "flickers," as the new silent movies were called. Many actors had trouble switching from stage to film, but Gladys, or Mary Pickford, as she now called herself, found it easy.

With her long blond curls, Mary became known as "America's Sweetheart." She charged a bigger fee for every movie she made. People were stunned that tiny, gentle-looking Mary was so demanding. But Mary was shrewd as well as sweet.

By 1919 the film studios couldn't afford her salary. That didn't stop Mary. She and some other actors got together and founded their own studio — United Artists (now part of MGM).

Mary was Hollywood's first superstar. While honeymooning in Europe with her actor husband, Douglas Fairbanks, in 1920, she was mobbed by fans. Once she was almost killed by the crowds. Mary won two Academy Awards, and in the late 1950s became famous for having one of the largest jewellery collections in the world.

DID YOU KNOW

By the time Mary Pickford was 24, she was Hollywood's first millionaire.

Céline Dion

Singer

Born: *Mar. 30, 1968, at Charlemagne, PQ*

The youngest of 14 children in a very musical family, Céline Dion recorded a demo tape when she was only 12. She sent it to René Angelil, a Quebec record producer and manager, who was amazed by her voice. René believed in Céline's talent so much that he mortgaged his house to pay for the recording of her first album.

He later became her husband.

Soon Céline was a star in Quebec. Then in 1983, while still a teenager, she became the first Canadian to earn a Gold Record in France. Céline's albums have sold millions, and she continues to win awards and honours around the world. Her success is due to her incredible voice, discipline and determination. Céline also helps raise awareness about cystic fibrosis, a respiratory disease that killed one of her nieces.

Emily Carr

Painter, writer

Born: *Dec. 13, 1871, at Victoria, BC*

Died: *Mar. 2, 1945, at Victoria, BC*

When Emily Carr was growing up, painting was considered a nice hobby for proper young ladies but not a serious career choice. Emily, however, longed to paint, especially the lush landscapes of British Columbia's west coast.

She was most inspired by Kwakiutl Native villages. Emily headed out alone by boat to paint village houses and totem poles. On one visit to Ucluelet, on the west coast of Vancouver Island, she was given the name "Klee Wyck," which means Laughing One.

Painting didn't earn Emily enough money to live on, so she rented out rooms in her Victoria house. Being a landlady took up a lot of time, leaving less for painting. But Emily didn't give up.

It wasn't until 1928, when Emily was 57, that people really started to notice her art. She had met the members of the Group of Seven (page 38) the year before, and they encouraged and helped her. Their inspiration motivated her to paint forests, shorelines and skies that shimmered with light and energy.

Emily loved animals and was always surrounded by dogs, cats, birds and even a pet monkey. During the summer, she would head off with her pets to her trailer (which she called The Elephant) to be closer to nature and create her art.

In 1937 Emily had a heart attack and was told to cut back on her painting. So she began writing — and became an award-winning writer. Her books are published in more than 20 languages and are read all over the world. But Emily is best known for her art. She is still Canada's most famous woman artist, and her paintings hang on gallery walls across the country.

> "WOODS AND SKIES OUT WEST ARE BIG. YOU CAN'T SQUEEZE THEM DOWN."
>
> — *Emily Carr*

Pitseolak Ashoona

Artist

Born: *1904 at Nottingham Island, NU*

Died: *May 28, 1983, at Cape Dorset, NU*

"I know I have had an unusual life," Pitseolak Ashoona once said, "being born in a skin tent and living to hear on the radio that two men have lived on the moon."

Pitseolak didn't begin drawing until she was in her fifties and needed to support her family. In her Arctic home, she drew monsters,

spirits and scenes from what she called "the old ways."

Always anxious to learn new skills and try new art tools, Pitseolak put them to good use, creating more than 7000 drawings and 250 prints in 20 years. The imagery and style of her art recall traditional Inuit life and have made her one of Canada's best-known Inuit artists. The energy and humour she put into her work makes her art still very popular.

Pauline Johnson

Poet, entertainer and Native rights activist

Born: *Mar. 10, 1861, on the Six Nations Indian Reserve at Oshweken, ON*

Died: *Mar. 7, 1913, at Vancouver, BC*

In Canada during the 1890s, women were expected to marry, have children and keep quiet about how they felt. Not Pauline Johnson. She toured all over North America and Britain, performing her poetry and speaking out passionately about Canada and Native rights. She made Canadians think about First Nations people, as well as themselves and their place in the world, and became Canada's most popular entertainer of the early 1900s.

The daughter of a Mohawk chief and an English mother, Pauline became famous as "The Mohawk Princess." She called herself *Tekahionwake* (you say it Dega-hee-yawn-wagay), meaning "double wampum" in Mohawk.

Pauline was the first Native poet to have her work published in Canada and one of the few women writers at the time who made a living from writing and performing. Attracting crowds and keeping their attention was easy for Pauline because she was a clever entertainer. She would often dress in Native costume and tell witty jokes or give dramatic recitations.

Proud of her Native heritage, Pauline wrote and spoke out in support of her culture. She is the only person ever buried in Stanley Park, her favourite spot in Vancouver.

> … And up on the hills against
>   the sky,
> A fir tree rocking its lullaby,
> Swings, swings,
> Its emerald wings,
> Swelling the song that my paddle
>   sings.
>
> — *from "The Song My Paddle Sings"*

Cornelius Krieghoff

Painter

Born: *June 19, 1815, at Amsterdam, Holland*

Died: *Mar. 8, 1872, at Chicago, MI, U.S.*

Cornelius Krieghoff studied painting in Europe, then arrived in Quebec in 1840. He soon became famous for his paintings of *habitants* (local farmers) and First Nations people. Cornelius's pictures told interesting stories, and

he knew which details to include to capture the richness — and harshness — of people's lives in Quebec at that time.

You can tell from Cornelius's art that he loved nature and people. He produced more than 2000 oil paintings during his life, all full of colour and energy. They were as popular then as they are now, and Cornelius has become known as a classic Canadian artist.

John McCrae

World War I was a nightmare for John McCrae. Although he'd been a doctor for many years and had already served in the South African (Boer) War, in this war he was surrounded by dead and dying soldiers. Every day he cared for hundreds of wounded men — but he couldn't get used to their terrible suffering.

The day after burying a friend on a battlefield in Belgium, John realized he couldn't help his friend or other dead soldiers, but he *could* tell of their lives in a poem. He could see blood-red poppies blowing in the wind in a nearby cemetery, and they inspired him to write "In Flanders Fields."

John didn't think the poem was very good and threw it away. But another officer found the poem and sent it to magazines and newspapers in England, where it was published on December 8, 1915. Because of John's poem, the poppy became the flower of remembrance for many countries, including Canada.

John died of pneumonia at a battle hospital in 1918. His poem was used on billboards in Canada to raise money for the war effort, and $400 million was collected — almost three times the hoped-for amount. "In Flanders Fields" is still recited around the world on Remembrance Day each year.

In Flanders fields the poppies blow
Between the crosses, row on row,
That mark our place, and in the sky
The larks, still bravely singing, fly
Scarce heard amid the guns below.

— *from "In Flanders Fields"*

Norval Morrisseau

Norval Morrisseau, or Copper Thunderbird as his name means in Ojibwa, grew up on a First Nations reserve in Ontario. He loved to go exploring in his canoe and visit ancient Native sites, especially ones that contained rock drawings called petroglyphs. When Norval was 19, he fell ill with tuberculosis, a serious lung

disease. One of his doctors suggested that he try painting while recovering.

Norval is famous for developing the Woodland Indian art style, now used by many Native artists. It's also known as "X-ray art" because it reveals what animals and people might look like inside their bodies, as well as how they look on the outside. His brightly coloured, high-energy paintings gained him a wide reputation. Today his work hangs in museums and galleries around the world.

The Group of Seven

Painters	
Formed: 1920	
Disbanded: 1933	

Between 1911 and 1913, a group of young men began to paint together. Franklin Carmichael, Lawren Harris, A.Y. Jackson, Frank (later Franz) Johnston, Arthur Lismer, J.E.H. MacDonald, Tom Thomson and F.H. Varley shared an idea for a new style of painting that captured Canada's spirit. Most of them earned money during the week by designing posters and ads. But on weekends and holidays they explored Canada's wilderness, creating small sketches with oil paints from which they created their larger, final paintings.

These artists used bright colours and rough brushstrokes to show how different Canada was from other countries. They knew they were doing something unusual, so they decided to show their art in a group, figuring that might help people accept it. They decided to call themselves the Group of Seven. (Tom Thomson had died in a canoe accident in 1917, leaving just seven artists.) The Group's first exhibition in Toronto in 1920 caused a huge commotion. One critic called the Group the Hot Mush School because he thought the paintings looked more like porridge than art. Others liked the fresh new way the Group pictured Canada.

The Group of Seven painted to show not only how parts of Canada looked but also how these natural areas made them feel. With a new sense of confidence and independence after World War I, Canadians soon accepted these artists who made such strong paintings of the country they loved.

As members left the Group, other painters — A.J. Casson, L.L. FitzGerald and Edwin Holgate — joined. Today you'll find paintings by Group of Seven members in every major gallery in Canada.

Time Line

1920	Franklin Carmichael, Lawren Harris, A.Y. Jackson, Frank Johnston, Arthur Lismer, J.E.H. MacDonald and Frederick H. Varley form the Group of Seven in Toronto
1920s	Members of the Group travel to the Prairies, Rockies, east and west coasts, and the Arctic to paint
1924	Frank Johnston leaves the Group
1926	A.J. Casson becomes a member of the Group of Seven
1931	Edwin Holgate joins the Group
	The Group of Seven holds its last art show
1932	J.E.H. MacDonald dies
	L.L FitzGerald is invited to join the Group of Seven
1933	The Group breaks up. The Canadian Group of Painters forms.

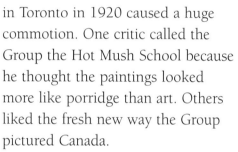

Frank Carmichael painted Autumn Hillside *in 1920. All the members of the Group of Seven liked to paint with strong, bright colours.*

1. Casson, 2. Varley, 3. Jackson,
4. Harris, 5. Carmichael,
6. Johnston, 7. Lismer,
8. MacDonald, 9. Fitzgerald,
10. Holgate, 11. Thomson

Franklin Carmichael

Unlike most of the Group of Seven, who used oil paint, often painted in watercolours
Born: May 4, 1890, at Orillia, ON
Died: Oct. 24, 1945, at Toronto, ON
Well-known painting: Mirror Lake

Alfred Joseph Casson

Painted small Ontario towns and never painted outside the province; joined the Group in 1926
Born: May 17, 1898, at Toronto, ON
Died: Feb. 20, 1992, at Toronto, ON
Well-known painting: The White Pine

Lionel LeMoine FitzGerald

Became known as the "Painter of the Prairies"; joined the Group in 1932
Born: Mar. 17, 1890, at Winnipeg, MB
Died: Aug. 7, 1956, at Winnipeg, MB
Well-known painting: Pembina Valley

Lawren Stewart Harris

Painted landscapes in a simple but powerful style, and also created portraits and abstracts
Born: Oct. 23, 1885, at Brantford, ON
Died: Jan. 29, 1970, at Vancouver, BC
Well-known painting: Above Lake Superior

Edwin Holgate

Best known for his paintings of people; joined the Group in 1930
Born: Aug. 19, 1892, at Allandale, ON
Died: May 21, 1977, at Montreal, PQ
Well-known painting: Ludivine

Alexander Young Jackson

A very popular member of the Group of Seven and its best spokesperson
Born: Oct. 3, 1882, at Montreal, PQ
Died: Apr. 5, 1974, at Kleinburg, ON
Well-known painting: Terre Sauvage

Frank Johnston

Painted with lots of energy and produced many works that sold well
Born: June 19, 1888, at Toronto, ON
Died: July 9, 1949, at Toronto, ON
Well known painting: Sunset in the Bush

Arthur Lismer

Became a famous art teacher of children
Born: June 27, 1885, at Sheffield, England
Died: Mar. 23, 1969, at Montreal, PQ
Well-known painting: A September Gale, Georgian Bay

James Edward Hervey MacDonald

Wrote many articles defending the Group's aims
Born: May 12, 1873, at Durham, England
Died: Nov. 26, 1932, at Toronto, ON
Well-known painting: The Tangled Garden

Thomas Thomson

Inspired the original members of the Group to explore Canada's wilderness areas
Born: Aug. 5, 1877, at Claremont, ON
Died: July 8, 1917, at Canoe Lake, ON
Well-known painting: The West Wind

Frederick Horsman Varley

Was an official war artist in World War I and was also known for his portraits
Born: Jan. 2, 1881, at Sheffield, England
Died: Sept. 8, 1969, at Toronto, ON
Well-known painting: Vera

DID YOU KNOW

In the 1920s, a Group of Seven painting might have sold for about $300. A few years ago, *Baffin Island* by Lawren Harris sold for more than $2 million.

GOVERNMENT

The desire to make their country a better place has driven many Canadians to get involved in politics or the justice system. For some Canadians that means working for people's rights as a politician or an activist. Others choose the world of law.

The great Canadians in this section stand out for a number of reasons. Without the Fathers of Confederation uniting the various provinces, we'd have a very different country today — or perhaps none at all. Other great Canadians have provided leadership as we've debated our future, or have challenged us to hold our heads higher in the world. Some of these politicians and leaders have opened the doors for a more equal system of government, in which all Canadians can participate.

Pierre Elliott Trudeau

Prime minister of Canada, 1968–1979 and 1980–1984

Born: Oct. 18, 1919, at Montreal, PQ

Died: Sept. 28, 2000, at Montreal, PQ

In 1968 "Trudeaumania" swept Canada. The man behind this craze was Pierre Elliott Trudeau, a Cabinet minister and a candidate for prime minister. Crowds gathered to hear him, get his autograph or touch him. Late that year, he was elected prime minister in an overwhelming victory.

Pierre didn't want special treatment for his home province of Quebec, but he *did* want it to be equal. He passed the Official Languages Act in 1969 declaring both French and English to be Canada's official languages.

In 1970 the Front de Libération du Québec (FLQ) kidnapped two men in Montreal. Pierre brought in the War Measures Act, which allowed people to be quickly arrested. All Canada watched as soldiers patrolled Montreal. When Pierre was asked how far he would go to preserve order, he said, "Just watch me!" The FLQ murdered one of their hostages before the October Crisis ended.

Perhaps Pierre's biggest accomplishment was bringing home Canada's constitution — the country's highest rules and laws. For years it had bothered him that the constitution could only be changed in Britain. (This dated back to when Canada was a British colony.) Some of the provinces opposed Pierre's efforts to bring these laws to Canada. But finally, on April 17, 1982, the Constitution Act and the Charter of Rights and Freedoms were proclaimed in Ottawa by Queen Elizabeth.

Smart, arrogant, charming, determined — Pierre was all these things, and he challenged Canadians as no other political leader ever has.

"CANADA WILL BE A STRONG COUNTRY WHEN CANADIANS OF ALL PROVINCES FEEL AT HOME IN ALL PARTS OF THE COUNTRY, AND WHEN THEY FEEL THAT ALL CANADA BELONGS TO THEM."

— *Pierre Trudeau*

Wilfrid Laurier

Prime minister of Canada, 1896–1911

Born: Nov. 20, 1841, at St-Lin, PQ

Died: Feb. 17, 1919, at Ottawa, ON

When Wilfrid Laurier became prime minister in 1896, Canadians were often divided into French vs. English, Roman Catholic vs. Protestant. Wilfrid longed for a united Canada. As well, Britain was still making a lot of decisions for Canada, and Wilfrid wanted Canada to take charge of its own future.

A skilful politician with lots of ambition and personality, Wilfrid was good at finding compromises between opposing groups. He was smart, handsome, charming and, more than

"THE TWENTIETH CENTURY BELONGS TO CANADA."

— *Wilfrid Laurier*

a century later, is still one of Canada's most popular prime ministers.

Canada went through a lot of changes while Wilfrid was prime minister. The Klondike gold rush started in 1896, and people swarmed into Canada's Northwest. Wilfrid's government encouraged settlers from Europe to begin new lives on the prairies. It also created the Royal Canadian Navy so that Canada did not have to rely on Britain for defence. Wilfrid proudly saw his country become more independent and strong.

Wilfrid's government was elected again and again. He was Canada's leader for 15 years, the longest unbroken term of any prime minister. Canada's first French-Canadian prime minister, Wilfrid still inspires Canadians.

Bertha Wilson

First woman appointed to the Supreme Court of Canada

Born: Sept. 18, 1923, at Kirkcaldy, Scotland

Died: Apr. 28, 2007, at Ottawa, ON

In 1982 Bertha Wilson became the first woman judge appointed to the Supreme Court of Canada, the country's top court. If people don't agree with the decision made by another court, the Supreme Court

is the last place they can take their court case.

Like many women who are the first to enter men's fields, Bertha faced prejudice and discrimination. Perhaps because of this, she had special sympathy for those who lack power in Canadian society.

Bertha was especially known for her creative and caring decisions in human rights and child custody cases. She also made important contributions to the Royal Commission on Aboriginal People.

Lester B. Pearson

Prime minister of Canada, 1963–1968

Born: Apr. 23, 1897, at Newtonbrook, ON

Died: Dec. 27, 1972, at Ottawa, ON

When Lester B. Pearson's squadron leader in World War I decided Lester was no name for a flying ace, he nicknamed the flier "Mike."

After the war, the easy-going and charming Mike became a history professor. Later, as a diplomat, he negotiated Canada's relationships with other countries. In 1945 he was at the founding of the United Nations (UN), a new organization he had worked hard to promote.

Mike became world famous in 1956 when he suggested a way to end fighting over the Suez Canal in Egypt. He proposed that the UN create an emergency force to send soldiers wherever they were needed, starting with Egypt. For this plan, he won a Nobel Prize (page 56).

In 1958 Mike became leader of the Liberal Party, and five years later was elected prime minister. Under his leadership, the government focused on how to keep Canada's dual French and English culture alive. Also, in 1965, Canada got its own flag. In 1967 Mike led Canadians in a celebration of 100 years of Confederation.

Lester B. Pearson is the only Canadian to win the Nobel Peace Prize. Today the Pearson Peace Medal is given to Canadians who, like Mike, try to make the world a more peaceful place.

"MAY THE LAND OVER WHICH THIS NEW FLAG FLIES REMAIN UNITED IN FREEDOM AND JUSTICE … INDUSTRIOUS, ENERGETIC, RESOLUTE, WISE, AND JUST IN THE GIVING OF SECURITY AND OPPORTUNITY EQUALLY TO ALL ITS CULTURES …"

— *Lester B. Pearson*

Tommy Douglas

Father of medicare

Born: Oct. 20, 1904, at Falkirk, Scotland

Died: Feb. 24, 1986, at Ottawa, ON

In 1911 seven-year-old Thomas Douglas had bone disease in one leg. His parents couldn't afford the surgery to save it, so Tommy faced amputation. His leg was spared when a doctor offered to operate for free. Tommy never forgot this experience and vowed to make sure that poverty would never stop people from getting medical care.

The Great Depression of 1929 to 1939 hit the people of Saskatchewan, where Tommy lived, especially hard. He decided the way to make changes was to get into politics. Because he was a spellbinding and witty speaker, people listened and, in 1935, elected him as a member of Canada's federal Parliament. Tommy switched to provincial politics in 1944 and was elected premier of Saskatchewan.

In 1961 Tommy returned to federal politics and became the first leader of the New Democratic Party. A year later, thanks to Tommy, medicare was brought in. For the first time, doctors were paid by the government, not the patients, so that all Canadians could get the care they needed.

Jeanne Sauvé

First woman Speaker of the House of Commons and Governor General

Born: *Apr. 26, 1922, at Prud'homme, SK*

Died: *Jan. 26, 1993, at Montreal, PQ*

There were many firsts in Jeanne Sauvé's life as a politician. In Ottawa's House of Commons, she was the first woman member of the Cabinet from Quebec and the first woman elected as Speaker (the person who oversees debates in Parliament). She also opened the first daycare centre on Parliament Hill. When Jeanne was appointed Governor General of Canada in 1984 — the first woman to hold the post — she called it "a magnificent breakthrough for women."

Before getting involved in politics, Jeanne was a journalist with a special interest in politics and women's rights. Later as a smart, energetic and efficient politician, she pushed Canada to become a world leader in technology.

Jeanne also loved sports and wanted to encourage more Canadians to get involved. She set up the Jeanne Sauvé Trophy for the world cup championship of women's field hockey. The Jeanne Sauvé Fair Play Award was started to encourage amateur athletes to play safely and avoid violence. Jeanne also began the Jeanne Sauvé Youth Foundation to motivate young people.

That world peace was so important to Jeanne Sauvé that when she was Governor General her coat of arms included a dove, the world symbol for peace.

Rosemary Brown

First Black woman to run for the leadership of a national political party

Born: *June 17, 1930, at Kingston, Jamaica*

Died: *Apr. 26, 2003, at Vancouver, BC*

When she came to Canada from Jamaica for university in 1950, Rosemary Brown found that no one wanted to be her roommate because of her skin colour. Later, it was tough for her to find a job or a place to live. Those experiences made her determined to make changes.

In 1972 Rosemary became the first Black woman elected to the British Columbia provincial legislature. Two years later, the New Democratic Party wanted a woman to run for the party's leadership and they asked Rosemary. Even though she lost, she raised awareness of women's and Black people's rights.

She once said "to be Black and female in a society which is both racist and sexist is to be in the unique position of having nowhere to go but up!" Stubborn but with a good sense of humour, Rosemary has helped groups working for human rights, peace and women's issues.

Louis Riel

Few Canadians have divided the country as Louis Riel did. Some people admired him for defending western Canada in the new nation, while others hated him for starting Canada's only civil war.

Louis was a leader of the Métis — people of First Nations and European descent — in the Red River Settlement, part of today's Manitoba. In 1868 Louis feared that the Hudson's Bay Company was about to hand over a huge area of Métis land to Canada. So Louis and the Métis stopped Canadian authorities from entering the settlement.

Strong and determined, Louis set up a Métis government to negotiate.

But the talks failed, and in 1869 that led to the Red River Rebellion. The Métis fought for their land and rights against Canadian settlers and soldiers.

The next year, the Canadian government recognized the rights of the Métis and created the province of Manitoba, with Louis as its leader. But during the Rebellion, Louis's government had hanged a man. Canada's government felt Louis was responsible, so he fled the country.

More and more, Louis felt he had a religious mission to lead the Métis. In 1885 he became involved in another battle at Duck Lake, Saskatchewan. This soon grew into the Northwest Rebellion. With the Métis far outnumbered, Louis turned himself in.

Louis went on trial for high treason. His defence lawyer wanted him to plead not guilty because of insanity, but he refused and was found guilty. Many people thought he should be spared, but on November 16, 1885, Louis was hanged. The justice — or injustice — of this event still causes arguments among Canadians.

> "I HAVE DEVOTED MY LIFE TO MY COUNTRY. IF IT IS NECESSARY FOR THE HAPPINESS OF MY COUNTRY THAT I SHOULD NOW CEASE TO LIVE, I LEAVE IT TO THE PROVIDENCE OF MY GOD."
>
> — *Louis Riel*

René Lévesque

As a journalist and later as a Liberal member of the Quebec legislature, René Lévesque was known for his commitment to Quebec.

Convinced that Quebeckers should take charge of their own destiny — and do it in their own language — René quit the Liberals in 1967. A year later, he was leading the Parti Québécois, the party that promoted Quebec's separation from the rest of Canada. He became premier of Quebec in 1976, and his government passed a controversial law (called Bill 101) to preserve French language and culture.

In a referendum (a vote by all citizens) in 1980, and again in 1995, Quebeckers chose to remain part of Canada. But René had made them think about their place in the country and feel proud of their culture. He also forced all Canadians to think about what their country means to them.

Agnes Macphail

First woman member of Parliament

Born: *Mar. 24, 1890, at Grey County, ON*

Died: *Feb. 13, 1954, at Toronto, ON*

A desire to help the farmers in her region got schoolteacher Agnes Macphail involved in politics. The year was 1919, and women had just won the right to run for Parliament. Agnes was the only woman elected to Canada's Parliament in 1921, during the first federal election in which women could vote.

Some people didn't know what to make of Canada's first woman member of Parliament. They made fun of Agnes's clothes and said she was dowdy, with no sense of humour. She hated that. But Agnes didn't give

up, and soon people came to respect her. She claimed that her parents had taught her to be persistent.

Agnes worked with many groups to help the underprivileged. To assist women in conflict with the law, she helped start the Elizabeth Fry Society in Canada. Because Agnes focused on fighting for the rights of women, the poor and people in prison, some politicians thought she was a real troublemaker.

Agnes left federal politics and in 1943 switched to provincial politics. She continued to work hard — in 1951 Agnes helped bring in a law that promised women of Ontario the same pay as men for the same work.

"I OWED IT TO MY FATHER THAT I WAS ELECTED TO PARLIAMENT IN THE FIRST PLACE, BUT I OWED IT TO MY MOTHER THAT I STUCK IT OUT ONCE I GOT THERE."

— *Agnes Macphail*

Cairine Wilson

Canada's first woman senator

Born: *Feb. 4, 1885, at Montreal, PQ*

Died: *Mar. 3, 1962, at Ottawa, ON*

When Cairine Wilson was appointed Canada's first woman senator in 1930, she knew she was in for a tough time. She told Prime Minister William Lyon Mackenzie King, who gave her the job, "You are going to make me the most hated woman in Canada."

Why was Cairine so worried? She figured the other senators wouldn't welcome a woman in the Senate. And she realized that most

Canadians thought Emily Murphy (page 12) should have been appointed instead, for her success in having women declared persons and therefore eligible to be senators.

But Cairine had helped get King elected prime minister, and he wanted to give her an important job to thank her. He also probably thought she would go along with everything he proposed. Not Cairine — she worked hard to improve life for women, immigrants and refugees, even when she had to disagree with the prime minister.

Cairine was also chairman of the Canadian National Committee on Refugees and the first woman from Canada appointed to the United Nations General Assembly.

The Fathers of Confederation

By the 1860s, the colonies in what is now Canada knew it was time for change. The United States was threatening to take them over, and Britain no longer wanted to pay to defend them. As well, the colonies weren't growing as quickly as they might because it was difficult for them to sell goods to each other —

transportation between them was extremely poor. They began to think of banding together to become stronger and more successful.

It took three conferences and almost three years, but finally on July 1, 1867, the new country of Canada was created. It consisted of the provinces of New Brunswick,

Nova Scotia, Ontario (formerly Canada West) and Quebec (Canada East). This union of colonies depended on the vision and determination of the Fathers of Confederation, who dreamed of a powerful new nation that would eventually stretch from the Atlantic Ocean to the Pacific.

The Most Famous Fathers of Confederation

George Brown (1818–1880) acted for Canada West in the Confederation talks. An excellent speaker, he was one of the first people to suggest uniting the colonies. Before becoming a politician, he founded Toronto's Globe newspaper, which later became The Globe and Mail.

Georges-Étienne Cartier (1814–1873) was a French-Canadian leader and a strong supporter of Confederation. He played an important role in persuading the French of Canada East to join the nation. With John A. Macdonald he was co-premier of Canada East and Canada West from 1857 to 1862.

Alexander Galt (1817–1893) represented English speakers in Canada East. He was a brilliant businessman and was strongly in favour of Confederation. He wanted a railway across the country and knew Confederation would make it easier to build one.

John A. Macdonald (1815–1891) *from Canada West played such a large part in Confederation that he was made Canada's first prime minister on July 1, 1867. He added five more provinces to Canada and began building a transcontinental railway to span the nation and strongly connect the provinces.*

Samuel L. Tilley (1818–1896) *was a businessman before he became a politician. He believed that Confederation could help the colonies prosper. As premier of New Brunswick, he also wanted a railway to connect the Maritimes to the other colonies.*

Thomas D'Arcy McGee (1825–1868) *was known as the best public speaker of his time. Feeling Canada was a better place to live than the United States, he supported Confederation to prevent the U.S. from taking over the colonies. He was one of the few politicians ever assassinated in Canada.*

Charles Tupper (1821–1915) *attended the Confederation meetings as premier of Nova Scotia and was strongly in favour of the union. In 1896 he became Canada's shortest-serving prime minister. When he died, he was the last survivor of the 36 Fathers of Confederation.*

The Other Fathers of Confederation

Adams G. Archibald (1814–1892)
Alexander Campbell (1822–1892)
F.B.T. Carter (1819–1900)
E.B. Chandler (1800–1880)
J.C. Chapais (1811–1885)
James Cockburn (1819–1883)
George Coles (1810–1875)
R.B. Dickey (1811–1903)
Charles Fisher (1808–1880)
J.H. Gray (1811–1887)
J.H. Gray (1814–1889)
T.H. Haviland (1822–1895)
W.A. Henry (1816–1888)
W.P. Howland (1811–1907)
J.M. Johnson (1818–1868)
Hector Langevin (1826–1906)
A.A. Macdonald (1829–1912)
Jonathan McCully (1809–1877)
William McDougall (1822–1905)
Peter Mitchell (1824–1899)
Oliver Mowat (1820–1903)
Edward Palmer (1809–1889)
W.H. Pope (1825–1879)
J.W. Ritchie (1808–1890)
Ambrose Shea (1815–1905)
W.H. Steeves (1814–1873)
Étienne P. Taché (1795–1865)
Edward Whelan (1824–1867)
R.D. Wilmot (1809–1891)

Twentieth-Century Fathers of Confederation

Joey Smallwood (1900–1991) and Paul Okalik (1964–) can also be considered Fathers of Confederation. Joey campaigned hard for Newfoundland to join Canada, and when it did in 1949, he became its first premier. Paul was the first premier of Nunavut, which became a Canadian territory in 1999.

"WHATEVER YOU DO, ADHERE TO THE UNION. WE ARE A GREAT COUNTRY, AND SHALL BECOME ONE OF THE GREATEST IN THE UNIVERSE IF WE PRESERVE IT …"

— *John A. Macdonald*

When Did They Join?

Here's when today's provinces and territories became part of Canada:

1867: New Brunswick
Nova Scotia
Ontario
Quebec
1870: Manitoba
Northwest Territories
1871: British Columbia

1873: Prince Edward Island
1898: Yukon Territory
1905: Alberta
Saskatchewan
1949: Newfoundland and Labrador
1999: Nunavut

SPORTS

When people think of Canada and athletics, one sport comes to mind — hockey. And it's true that many of our best-known athletes are hockey players. But Canadians excel at many sports, both winter and summer. We're also famous sports innovators.

Canadian athletes have changed the way many sports are played and raised the level for players around the world. There's no prouder moment for a Canadian athlete than to compete in a world championship and hear Canada's national anthem played to honour a gold-medal win.

Wayne Gretzky

Hockey player

Born: *Jan. 26, 1961, at Brantford, ON*

No wonder he's been called the "Great One" ever since he was a kid. When he was 10, Wayne Gretzky scored 378 goals in just 68 games. At 17, he was the youngest player in professional sport in North America. He has set or tied 61 National Hockey League (NHL) records and is the league's all-time leading scorer, with 2857 points. Wayne is the only player to reach 2000 career points.

Like most Canadian kids, Wayne began playing hockey on a rink his dad had flooded their backyard in Brantford, Ontario. Wayne credits his father with supporting his desire to play hockey and helping him without

"YOU MISS 100 PERCENT OF THE SHOTS YOU DON'T TAKE."

— *Wayne Gretzky*

pushing too much. Wayne would shoot and skate for hours — he loved it so much that it never seemed like practising to him. When he played in the NHL, he would exhaust his teammates with his long practices.

Wayne wasn't big, and his style wasn't smooth, but he had an accurate shot and an incredible instinct for the game. He seemed to see plays happen in slow motion and so could anticipate where the puck was heading. Players talked about the area behind the goal as being "Gretzky's office," because he liked to set up plays from behind the net. And Wayne had the greatest pass in hockey history — his record number of 1963 assists proves it.

Although proud of his hockey records, Wayne is even more pleased that he has raised the profile of hockey around the world. And he was especially proud to be executive director of Canada's men's Olympic hockey team in 2002 and lead them on to the gold medal.

When Wayne played for the NHL's Edmonton Oilers during the 1985–86 season, he scored 215 points, still a record.

Marilyn Bell

Long-distance swimmer

Born: *Nov. 19, 1937, at Toronto, ON*

In 1954 the Canadian National Exhibition promised an American woman $10 000 dollars to swim the 51.5 km (32 mi.) across Lake Ontario. Marilyn Bell, a 16-year-old Toronto schoolgirl, decided to try, too, even though she wasn't offered any money. "As corny as it sounds," Marilyn later said, "I did it for Canada."

Just before midnight on September 8, the swimmers slipped into the chilly water off Youngstown, New York. The more experienced American had to quit, but Marilyn's fighting spirit kept her going. It took almost 21 long, cold hours, but when she touched shore in Toronto, she became the first person to swim across Lake Ontario.

One year later, in 1955, Marilyn was the youngest person to swim the English Channel, and the next year to cross the Juan de Fuca Strait in southern British Columbia.

Jamie Salé & David Pelletier

Pairs figure skaters

Jamie Salé

Born: *Apr. 21, 1977, at Calgary, AB*

David Pelletier

Born: *Nov. 22, 1974, at Sayabec, PQ*

Crowds gasped in delight as skaters Jamie Salé and David Pelletier performed their long program at the 2002 Winter Olympic Games. The pair's amazing lifts, throws and spirit convinced everyone that these skaters would win the gold medal.

But Jamie and David won silver instead — a judging scandal robbed them of a first-place finish. Still, the pair impressed everyone with their grace and sportsmanship. They kept smiling through the investigation and finally received their gold medals.

How does David explain their success? "When I ... skate with Jamie and I give her my hand, it's electricity and there is magic there."

Tom Longboat

Long-distance runner

Born: *July 4, 1887, on the Six Nations Indian Reserve, at Oshweken, ON*

Died: *Jan. 9, 1949, on the Six Nations Indian Reserve, at Oshweken, ON*

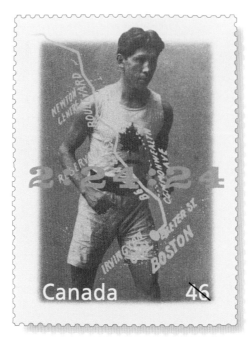

Spectacular finishing sprints made Thomas Longboat one of the world's greatest runners. He could summon a burst of energy at the end of a long race when his competitors could barely stay on their feet. His fans would go wild.

Born on an Ontario reserve, Tom had the talent to take over any race he was in, but off the track his life was tough. He often had fights with his managers over his training. He faced criticism and racist insults because he was a Native person. But nothing slowed him down — he just

kept winning. Because of his skin colour and swiftness, he came to be known as the "Bronze Mercury." Mercury is the Roman god of travel and the gods' messenger, who has wings on his heels.

Despite earning lots of money from racing, Tom quit to fight in World War I. He served as a dispatch runner, speeding messages and orders between groups of soldiers. He was wounded twice and once declared dead. But he managed to recover and kept running messages, as well as competing in races when he could.

During his athletic career, Tom won countless marathons, broke many speed records and became famous around the world.

Tom Longboat began running when he was a kid and practised by chasing cows.

Ned Hanlan

Rower

Born: *July 12, 1855, at Toronto, ON*

Died: *Jan. 4, 1908, at Toronto, ON*

The first Canadian athlete to become an internationally famous world champion, Toronto's Edward "Ned" Hanlan is still known as one

of the greatest scullers (rowers) ever. Ned was much smaller than most of his opponents, but so fast that he could build up a huge early lead, leaving the other rowers exhausted

and discouraged. He had great technique and a long, smooth stroke.

When Ned became world rowing champion in 1880, rowing was extremely popular around the world. Crowds mobbed him and showered him with gifts wherever he went. In all, Ned won more than 300 races during his sculling career.

Barbara Ann Scott

> **Figure skater**
>
> *Born: May 9, 1928, at Ottawa, ON*

By age nine, skater Barbara Ann Scott was practising seven hours every day in Ottawa. Her training paid off the next year when she became the youngest Canadian to pass the gold-medal figures test. That was just the beginning of an incredible skating career.

Barbara Ann was a graceful skater with excellent technique. But what really set her apart from other competitors was her love of the sport and her ability to concentrate during competition. It's hard to believe, but when she was skating in the 1940s, competitions were held outdoors. Barbara Ann was able to focus on her graceful routines despite rough ice, planes flying overhead or other distractions.

The first North American skater to win Olympic and World gold medals, and still the only Canadian to win Olympic gold in women's figure skating, Barbara Ann inspired many Canadians to try the sport. She became known as "Canada's Sweetheart," and many little girls treasured special Barbara Ann dolls designed to look just like Canada's skating star.

Barbara Ann Scott was the first woman to be voted Canada's outstanding athlete of the year, and she won this honour a record three times.

Bobbie Rosenfeld

> **All-round athlete**
>
> *Born: Dec. 28, 1905, in Russia*
>
> *Died: Nov. 14, 1969, at Toronto, ON*

In 1925 a very unusual team competed in the Ontario Ladies Track and Field Championship. The team won first and second prizes in discus, hurdles, long jump and javelin as well as various races. What was so unusual about this team? It had only one member — Fanny "Bobbie" Rosenfeld.

This incredible natural athlete reached her peak at the 1928 Olympic Games, winning a gold and a silver medal in track. These victories meant a lot to Bobbie because it was the first year women were allowed to compete in track-and-field events at the Olympics.

Bobbie had a good sense of humour and loved to compete in front of a large crowd. In 1949 she was honoured by being named Canada's top woman athlete of the first half of the 20th century.

Maurice Richard

Hockey player

Born: Aug. 4, 1921, at Montreal, PQ

Died: May 27, 2000, at Montreal, PQ

What a day! Maurice Richard worked for hours moving furniture, including a piano, into his new house. That night he had to play hockey with the Montreal Canadiens. Most people would have been too exhausted, but Maurice not only played — he scored five goals and three assists to win the game and set a National Hockey League (NHL) record.

Maurice was nicknamed the "Rocket" because of his speed on the ice. One of the highest scorers and most intense players in NHL history, he terrified his opponents. He was captain of the Canadiens, and his message to his players before every game was, "Let's go out and win it."

The Rocket was so passionate about hockey that he often lost his temper. In March 1955, he attacked another player, punched a linesman and was suspended for the rest of the season. His loyal fans were furious and the next night rioted in the streets of Montreal, the worst riot in Canadian sports history.

In the 1952 Stanley Cup semifinals, Maurice was carried off the ice unconscious after a collision. But with just four minutes left in the tie game he returned, blood seeping from his stitches, to score the game-winning goal. During his career, the Rocket played on eight Stanley Cup-winning teams and was also the first player to score 50 goals in 50 games.

DID YOU KNOW

The Maurice Richard Trophy is awarded each year to the NHL's top goal scorer.

Louis Cyr

Strongman

Born: Oct. 10, 1863, at St-Cyprien-de-Napierville, PQ

Died: Nov. 10, 1912, at St-Jean-de-Matha, PQ

In 1895 Louis Cyr lifted on his back a platform holding 18 large men — a weight of 1967 kg (4336 lb.). With one finger, Quebec's strongman could lift 272 kg (600 lb.)!

Louis worked as a lumberjack and policeman before he became a weightlifter. Feats of strength were extremely popular in his day, and Louis took part in many challenge matches. He was never defeated.

Once a horse was tied to each of his huge arms, but no matter how hard the horses tried to drag Louis in opposite directions, he was able to hold them at a standstill.

Nancy Greene

Skier

Born: *May 11, 1943, at Ottawa, ON*

Almost as soon as she could walk, Nancy Greene learned to ski. She loved the sport and was fast, determined and brave.

Nancy didn't begin serious racing until she was 14. She was good enough to compete in her first Olympics just two years later. Although she finished 22nd in her event — the giant slalom — she wasn't discouraged. If anything, she was more determined than ever.

Nancy's daring style caused her a lot of serious injuries. These setbacks made her realize that she would have to ski with more control. It worked. When World Cup skiing began its first season in 1966–67, Nancy placed first with four giant-slalom victories, plus two in slalom and one in downhill.

Nancy won the World Cup the next year as well. At the 1968 Winter Olympic Games, she made Canadians proud with a gold-medal win in giant slalom and a silver in slalom. To this day, no Canadian skier has won as many medals and awards as Nancy has.

With her quick smile and bright personality, Nancy has always been a favourite with the media. And she's popular with kids as well — her Nancy Greene Ski League has introduced young skiers across the country to the sport she loves so much and promotes so well.

> "YOU HAVE TO HAVE A REAL LOVE OF YOUR SPORT TO CARRY YOU THROUGH ALL THE BAD TIMES ..."
>
> — *Nancy Greene*

Silken Laumann

Rower

Born: *Nov. 14, 1964, at Mississauga, ON*

While training in her racing shell just two months before the 1992 Olympic Games, rower Silken Laumann had a bad accident — she broke her ankle and shredded muscles in her leg. Her doctors told her it would take her at least six months to recover, but Silken was determined to take part in the Olympics. She amazed the world when she went on to win bronze for rowing at the Games. Since then, she has won many medals, including, in 1996, an Olympic silver.

"You have to find a balance between working toward your goals of tomorrow and today," says Silken, whose mother named her for her silky hair. Today Silken works with Right to Play to help children in refugee camps around the world.

James Naismith

Inventor of basketball

Born: *Nov. 6, 1861, at Almonte, ON*

Died: *Nov. 28, 1939, at Lawrence, KS, U.S.*

What a challenge! Teacher James Naismith had just 14 days to invent a game for students when they couldn't exercise outside. He tried indoor soccer, football and lacrosse, but all were too dangerous.

James's new idea began with a large ball. Players would have to pass the ball, not run with it. The goal would be up high so the players couldn't block it with their bodies. Any rough conduct would earn a penalty. James loved lacrosse, so he gave his teams the same number of players.

The students tested the new game in December 1891. A janitor nailed up a peach basket at either end of the gym. Each time a player tossed the ball into the basket, the game had to stop while the janitor retrieved the ball. Even so, the players loved the game. Eventually someone decided to cut the bottoms out of the baskets.

James didn't have a name for his game. Some of the students suggested Naismith-ball, but he preferred another name — basketball.

DID YOU KNOW

James Naismith originally asked for boxes to be nailed up as goals in his game. Can you imagine playing "boxball"?

Jacques Plante

Hockey player

Born: *Jan. 17, 1929, near Mount Carmel, PQ*

Died: *Feb. 26, 1986, at Geneva, Switzerland*

When he was injured in an NHL game in November 1959, goalie Jacques Plante refused to return to the ice unless his coach allowed him to wear a mask. At that time, goalies didn't wear masks and often got hit in the face by pucks. Jacques wore his mask, his team won the game and soon many goalies imitated him.

The pride of the Montreal Canadiens, Jacques was an innovator in other ways, too. He was the first goalie to come out of his net to pass the puck up the ice to a teammate or to slip behind the goal and shoot the puck to a defenceman. Knitting long underwear, keeping notes on opponents' skills and blowing the crowd kisses were just a few of the unusual habits that endeared him to fans.

Jacques won the NHL's best goalie award a record seven times and played on six Stanley Cup-winning teams. He is still one of the few goalies ever to win the NHL's trophy for most valuable player.

Gordie Howe

Hockey player

Born: *Mar. 31, 1928, at Floral, SK*

To earn the nickname "Mr. Hockey," you have to be incredibly good, and Gordon Howe was. Not only was he one of the greatest hockey players of his time, but he's also one of the best professional athletes ever.

Gordie was strong and quick and could make the puck fly with his incredibly fast wrist shot. In 1977 he became the first NHL player ever to score 1000 points.

On the ice, Gordie wasn't afraid to take penalties and get tough — over his career he needed 500 stitches in his face alone. Off the ice, he was a modest and kind superstar who would spend

hours signing autographs for fans.

Many of the records Gordie set have since been broken. But it's unlikely anyone will topple his career records for most NHL games (1767) and seasons (26), almost all played with the Detroit Red Wings. He played hockey into his fifties and even had the thrill of playing with his two sons. It was the first time in professional team sports that a father had played with one son, let alone two!

DID YOU KNOW

Gordie Howe was among the top five scorers in the NHL for 20 straight seasons (few NHL players even last 20 seasons).

Lionel Conacher

All-round athlete and politician

Born: *May 24, 1902, at Toronto, ON*

Died: *May 26, 1954, at Ottawa, ON*

Baseball, boxing, football, hockey, lacrosse, track and wrestling — Lionel Conacher was a star at them all. Highlights of his career include winning the Canadian light-heavyweight boxing national championship in 1920, leading the Toronto Argonauts to win the Grey Cup in 1921 and playing rough-and-tough defence in the NHL in the 1930s. As well as being strong and fast, Lionel was aggressive and determined.

But Lionel was interested in more than sports. He entered politics in 1937 and became a member of the Ontario provincial Parliament and later the federal government.

Canada's Nobel Prize Winners

Since 1901, Nobel Prizes have been awarded to top achievers around the world in chemistry, literature, medicine, peace and physics. A prize for economics — the study of how things are made, distributed and bought — was added in 1969. The Nobel award consists of a gold medal, below, as well as a cash prize of about $1.4 million. Winners join a special group of world-famous thinkers and researchers.

Canada's first Nobel Prize came in 1923 for the discovery of insulin. Frederick Banting shared the prize with John Macleod, who had provided the space and equipment for the insulin experiments. Banting split his prize money with Charles Best, and Macleod shared his with James Collip, another key member of the team. (See page 20 for more about Banting and Best.)

Since then Canadians have won the Nobel Prize for work in fields ranging from genetics (Sidney Altman, 1989) to how atoms behave in solids (Bertram Brockhouse, 1994). In 1993 Michael Smith and his colleague won the chemistry award for a genetic engineering technique that lets researchers better understand how cancer and virus genes work.

Gerhard Herzberg won the Nobel Prize in 1971 for his research on the structure of molecules. In 1986 John Polanyi won with two others for their work on how chemical processes happen. New investigations into electrons (small particles in atoms) won the 1990 physics prize for a trio including Canadian Richard Taylor.

Canadians have won Nobel Prizes in other areas besides science. Lester B. Pearson (1897–1972) (page 42) won the Nobel Peace Prize in 1957 for encouraging world peace and helping to found the United Nations. In 1999 Robert Mundell (1932–) won the economics prize for his theory about international money systems.

(page 42)

DID YOU KNOW

Alfred Nobel, after whom the Nobel Prize is named, invented dynamite in 1866 and made a fortune building companies and labs in more than 20 countries around the world.

Being honoured with a Nobel Prize can make quite a difference to the lives of winners. It also makes Canadians proud to have such remarkable achievers making discoveries that improve life not just in Canada, but around the world.

Canada's Nobel Prize Winners

Frederick Banting (1891–1941)...........Medicine 1923, shared
John Macleod (1876–1935)................Medicine 1923, shared
Lester B. Pearson (1897–1972)............Peace 1957
Gerhard Herzberg (1904–1999)...........Chemistry 1971
John Polanyi (1929–).....................Chemistry 1986, shared
Sidney Altman (1939–)....................Chemistry 1989, shared
Richard Taylor (1929–)...................Physics 1990, shared
Michael Smith (1932–2000)...............Chemistry 1993, shared
Bertram Brockhouse (1918–2003).......Physics 1994, shared
Robert Mundell (1932–)..................Economics, 1999

Robert Mundell (left), Gerhard Herzberg (right) and Lester B. Pearson (page 42) are the only Canadian Nobel Prize winners whose awards were not shared.

MORE GREAT CANADIANS

There are so many great Canadians who are important for so many different reasons that it's impossible to fit them all into one book. But here are another 35 outstanding people you should meet. How many other great Canadians do you know?

Emma Albani (1847–1930) was the first Canadian opera singer to become famous around the world. She had an exceptionally beautiful voice that thrilled her audiences and won her the friendship of Queen Victoria queen of Britain and the Commonwealth.

Margaret Atwood (1939–) is a world-famous writer and poet. Her books have been translated into more than 20 languages and won many awards in Canada and other countries. She has also fought against censorship and defended the rights of writers around the world.

Henri Bourassa (1868–1952) founded Montreal's *Le Devoir*, one of Canada's most important newspapers. He was also a politician who felt Canada should be more independent from Britain, and a champion of French language rights and culture in Canada.

Lincoln Alexander (1922–) made headlines as the first Black Canadian to serve in Canada's Parliament, in Cabinet and as Ontario's Lieutenant-Governor. His work with youth and in education has won him many awards.

Jean Augustine (1937–) is the first Black woman in Canada's Parliament and in the Cabinet. This energetic, former school principal is especially concerned with social justice and women's issues.

Jim Carrey (1962–), right, & **Mike Myers (1963–)**, left, are actors and comedians who have created hilarious characters and brought a zany humour to the movie screens of the world.

Leonard Cohen (1934–) was known for his poetry before he became a singer and songwriter. His trademark low, raspy monotone and poetic lyrics have made him famous around the world, and artists from many countries have recorded his melancholy songs.

Arthur Currie (1875–1933) was the first Canadian to become a general and was the leading Canadian general of World War I. He planned and carried out a number of important battles — including the famous Vimy Ridge in France — that helped bring about the defeat of the Germans and the end of the war.

Arthur Erickson (1924–) is a Vancouver architect who has designed impressive buildings in Canada and around the world, including Simon Fraser University in Burnaby, British Columbia. He prefers simple materials, such as concrete, and uses them to create dramatic structures.

Alex Colville (1920–) is one of Canada's best-known painters. He paints his family, pets and landscapes in a style known as magic realism. This style makes ordinary people and places seem extraordinary, and encourages viewers to look at everyday things in a new way.

The Dionne Quintuplets (born in 1934, three are still alive) were the world's first quintuplets — five babies born at the same time. Up to 6000 people a day came to watch Annette, Cécile, Émilie, Marie and Yvonne play at "Quintland" close to their home near North Bay, Ontario.

Michael J. Fox (1961–) is an actor from Edmonton, Alberta, who starred in movies such as *Back to the Future* and the TV sitcoms *Family Ties* and *Spin City*. He has become known for his fight against Parkinson's, a disease which breaks down the nervous system and has no cure. Despite his illness, Michael works hard to raise awareness of Parkinson's and money for research.

Northrop Frye (1912–1991)

was one of Canada's greatest thinkers. While a professor at the University of Toronto, he wrote books that helped people see literature and the Bible in a new way.

John Kenneth Galbraith (1908–2006) was one of Canada's best-known economists (a person who studies how things are made, distributed and bought). His books and articles on economics have made the subject understandable to the general public.

James Gosling (1956–) created Java, a universal computer language that allows electronic equipment, such as cell phones and VCRs, to "talk" to each other.

Wilfred Grenfell (1865–1940) was a doctor and missionary in Newfoundland and Labrador. He made yearly visits to isolated communities in a hospital ship, helping thousands of patients. He also established hospitals and remote nursing stations along the coastlines. The International Grenfell Association continues his work.

Grey Owl (1888–1938) was the most famous North American Native person of his time. He wrote books and spoke in Canada and Britain about his love of nature and animals and the need to preserve the environment. After he died, it was discovered he was actually an Englishman called Archie Belaney. But he is still admired for his work as a conservationist.

Adelaide Hoodless (1857–1910)

founded the Women's Institute in 1897 after her baby son died from drinking bad milk. She wanted to prevent future accidents by teaching women to be skilled homemakers. Today, more than eight million women around the world belong to the Women's Institute. Adelaide also helped found the National Council of Women of Canada, the Victorian Order of Nurses and the Young Women's Christian Association (YWCA) of Canada.

Frances Ann Hopkins (1838–1918) canoed with her husband through Canada's wilderness, painting voyageurs at work. She had a keen eye and left an accurate and valuable record of life in the late 1800s. Frances's art often included herself and her husband, who worked for the Hudson's Bay Company. It was unusual for a woman to travel through the wilderness at that time, but Frances loved painting the hard-working fur traders.

Kenneth Colin Irving (1899–1992), New Brunswick's greatest businessman, was known as "K.C." He owned Canada's largest oil refinery, as well as shipyards; railway, bus and truck companies; gas stations; lumber companies; newspapers; and radio and TV stations.

Henry Kelsey (1667–1724), in 1690, became the first European to set foot in present-day Saskatchewan. Before becoming the Hudson's Bay Company's chief fur trader in charge of trading posts, he explored the prairies with the help of Native guides.

Calixa Lavallée (1842–1891) was a French-Canadian composer and musician who wrote the music for "O Canada!" in 1880. The French lyrics to Canada's national anthem were written by Adolphe-Basile Routhier, and Robert Stanley Weir added the English lyrics in 1908.

Stephen Leacock (1869–1944) was a professor, humour writer and one of the first Canadian writers to become world famous. The Stephen Leacock Medal for Humour is awarded every year in his honour for the funniest book written by a Canadian.

John McIntosh (1777–1845) discovered the crisp red apple that's named after him. He found trees that yielded  the apple on his own farm in Dundela, Ontario. McIntosh apple trees are very popular because they produce lots of fruit and grow in many climates.

Marshall McLuhan (1911–1980) was a philosopher of communications who became famous around the world. He wrote about how the invention of the printing press changed the world hundreds of years ago, and how mass media — television,  radio, newspapers, advertising — affect people in today's world.

Joni Mitchell (1943–) has won awards around the world for her unique guitar style, interesting song lyrics and light, high voice. She is one of Canada's best-known singers and songwriters and has written some of pop's most famous songs.

Susanna Moodie (1803–1885) was one of Canada's first female writers. Her writing is clever and fun, but shows great sensitivity. *Roughing It in the Bush,* her most famous book, describes her life as a British pioneer in Ontario's wilderness. **Catharine Parr Traill (1802–1899)**, Susanna's sister, was also a pioneer and a writer. In addition to her books for adults, Catharine wrote the first Canadian adventure novel for kids.

Poundmaker (1842–1886), whose Native name was Pitikwahanapiwiyin, was a Cree chief, skilled speaker and peacekeeper. His warriors clashed with government forces in the Northwest Rebellion of 1885 (page 44). Even though Poundmaker was not directly involved and protested that he was innocent, he was jailed for treason.

Mordecai Richler (1931–2001) won many awards for the books he wrote for both adults and kids. His popular children's book *Jacob Two-Two and the Hooded Fang* was made into a movie. One of Canada's most important fiction writers, he was especially known for his humorous and witty writing about life in the Jewish neighbourhoods of Montreal.

Charles Saunders (1867–1937) developed Marquis wheat, an early-ripening wheat that gave a good yield and made excellent bread. It doubled the area of prairie land where wheat could be grown and made Canada a major wheat producer.

David Suzuki (1936–) is an award-winning scientist, environmentalist, writer and TV host. He explains science in an interesting way that people find easy to understand. David first became famous for his work in genetics, the study of heredity.

Harriet Tubman (1820–1913) led hundreds of enslaved Black people to freedom along the Underground Railroad. This secret network of people helped slaves escape from southern American states, where slavery was legal, to freedom in northern states and Canada. Harriet fought hard for Black people's rights.

Joseph Tyrrell (1858–1957) found the first dinosaur bones near Drumheller, Alberta, in 1884. The area is now one of the world's most important collecting areas for dinosaur remains. He was a scientist and explorer who led expeditions across northern and western Canada. The Royal Tyrrell Museum at Drumheller is named after Joseph.

Jean Vanier (1928–) is a spiritual leader who set up L'Arche, a home for people with mental disabilities, in 1964. Jean challenges others to share their lives with handicapped people, as he does, and to learn from them. Now there are over 100 L'Arche communities around the world.

Madeleine de Verchères (1678–1747) was just 14 years old when she defended her settlement near Montreal against an attack by Iroquois warriors. With the help of only a few settlers, she fooled the invaders into thinking the fort was full of soldiers. Her quick thinking saved the community.

Time Line

Great Canadians	Date	Canadian Events
John Cabot (1449/50–1498/99) (p. 15)	**1450**	
Jacques Cartier (1491–1557) (p. 14)	1497	Cabot lands on Newfoundland
Martin Frobisher (1535/1539–1594) (p. 16)	**1500**	
	1534–42	Cartier explores Canada
	1535	Canada gets its name from Huron-Iroquois word for settlement, *Kanata*
Samuel de Champlain (1570–1635) (p. 15)	**1550**	
Henry Hudson (1570–1611) (p. 16)	1576–78	Frobisher's three voyages to the Arctic
Adam Dollard des Ormeaux (1635–1660) (p. 11)	**1600**	
	1605	Port-Royal built by French
	1608	Champlain founds Quebec
	1610	Hudson explores Hudson Bay
Henry Kelsey (1667–1724) (p. 60)	**1650**	
Madeleine de Verchères (1678–1747) (p. 61)	1670	Hudson's Bay Company founded
Alexander Mackenzie (1764–1820) (p. 17)	**1750**	
Tecumseh (1768–1813) (p. 11)	1759	Battle of Plains of Abraham
Isaac Brock (1769–1812) (p. 8)	1791	Constitutional Act creates Upper and Lower Canada
David Thompson (1770–1857) (p. 17)	1793	Alexander Mackenzie reaches Pacific Ocean overland
Laura Secord (1775–1868) (p. 8)		
Simon Fraser (1776–1862) (p. 18)		
John McIntosh (1777–1845) (p. 60)		
John Franklin (1786–1847) (p. 18)		
Samuel Cunard (1787–1865) (p. 27)		
Josiah Henson (1789–1883) (p. 10)		
Abraham Gesner (1797–1864) (p. 23)		
William Logan (1798–1875) (p. 21)		
Catharine Parr Traill (1802–1899) (p. 60)	**1800**	
Susanna Moodie (1803–1885) (p. 60)	1812	Red River Settlement begins
Cornelius Krieghoff (1815–1872) (p. 36)	1812–14	War of 1812
John A. Macdonald (1815–1891) (p. 47)	1830s–60s	Underground Railroad
Donald Smith (1820–1914) (p. 29)	1837–38	Rebellions in Lower and Upper Canada
Harriet Tubman (1820–1913) (p. 61)	1841	Upper and Lower Canada are joined to create Province of Canada
Hart Massey (1823–1896) (p. 28)		
Mary Ann Shadd (1823–1893) (p. 10)		
Sandford Fleming (1827–1915) (p. 21)		
Emily Stowe (1831–1903) (p. 25)		
Timothy Eaton (1834–1907) (p. 27)		
Frances Ann Hopkins (1838–1918) (p. 59)		
Wilfrid Laurier (1841–1919) (p. 41)		
Calixa Lavallée (1842–1891) (p. 60)		
Poundmaker (1842–1886) (p. 61)		
William Van Horne (1843–1915) (p. 29)		
Louis Riel (1844–1885) (p. 44)		
Emma Albani (1847–1930) (p. 57)		
Alexander Graham Bell (1847–1922) (p. 22)		
William Osler (1849–1919) (p. 25)		
Sam Steele (1849–1919) (p. 9)		
Leonora Howard King (1851–1925) (p. 24)	**1850**	
Alphonse Desjardins (1854–1920) (p. 26)	1858	Fraser River gold rush begins
Ned Hanlan (1855–1908) (p. 50)	1864	The Fathers of Confederation begin meeting
Adelaide Hoodless (1857–1910) (p. 59)	1867	Dominion of Canada formed
Joseph Tyrrell (1858–1957) (p. 61)	1869–70	The Red River Rebellion
Pauline Johnson (1861–1913) (p. 36)	1870	Hudson's Bay Company sells its territory to Canada
James Naismith (1861–1939) (p. 54)		Manitoba becomes Canada's fifth province
Louis Cyr (1863–1912) (p. 52)	1871	British Columbia becomes Canada's sixth province
Wilfred Grenfell (1865–1940) (p. 59)	1873	Prince Edward Island becomes Canada's seventh province
Reginald Fessenden (1866–1932) (p. 22)	1874	The North West Mounted Police made the official police force in the Canadian west
Charles Saunders (1867–1937) (p. 61)		
Henri Bourassa (1868–1952) (p. 57)	1885	Northwest Rebellion
Stephen Leacock (1869–1944) (p. 60)		Canadian Pacific Railway completed

Emily Carr (1871–1945) (p. 35)
Sam McLaughlin (1871–1972) (p. 28)
John McCrae (1872–1918) (p. 37)
Lucy Maud Montgomery (1874–1942) (p. 32)
Arthur Currie (1875–1933) (p. 58)
Elizabeth Arden (1878–1966) (p. 30)
Max Aitken (1879–1964) (p. 30)
Cairine Wilson (1885–1962) (p. 45)
Tom Longboat (1887–1949) (p. 50)
Grey Owl (1888–1938) (p. 59)
Norman Bethune (1890–1939) (p. 24)
Agnes Macphail (1890–1954) (p. 45)
Frederick Banting (1891–1941) (p. 20)
Mary Pickford (1892–1979) (p. 34)
Billy Bishop (1894–1956) (p. 9)
Roy Thomson (1894–1976) (p. 31)
Lester B. Pearson (1897–1972) (p. 42)
Floyd Chalmers (1898–1993) (p. 31)
Charles Best (1899–1978) (p. 20)
Kenneth Colin Irving (1899–1992) (p. 60)

Lionel Conacher (1902–1954) (p. 55)
Pitseolak Ashoona (1904–1983) (p. 35)
Tommy Douglas (1904–1986) (p. 42)
Bobbie Rosenfeld (1905–1969) (p. 51)
Armand Bombardier (1907–1964) (p. 23)
John Kenneth Galbraith (1908–2006) (p. 59)
Marshall McLuhan (1911–1980) (p. 60)
Northrop Frye (1912–1991) (p. 59)
Pierre Elliott Trudeau (1919–2000) (p. 40)
Alex Colville (1920–) (p. 58)
The Group of Seven (1920–1933) (p. 38)
Maurice Richard (1921–2000) (p. 52)
Lincoln Alexander (1922–) (p. 57)
René Lévesque (1922–1987) (p. 44)
Jeanne Sauvé (1922–1993) (p. 43)
Bertha Wilson (1923–2007) (p. 41)
Arthur Erickson (1924–) (p. 58)
Oscar Peterson (1925–) (p. 33)
The Famous Five (1927–1929) (p.12)
Gordie Howe (1928–) (p. 55)
Barbara Ann Scott (1928–) (p. 51)
Jean Vanier (1928–) (p. 61)
Jacques Plante (1929–1986) (p. 54)
Rosemary Brown (1930–2003) (p. 43)
Mordecai Richler (1931–2001) (p. 61)
Glenn Gould (1932–1982) (p. 33)
Norval Morrisseau (1932–) (p. 37)
Leonard Cohen (1934–) (p. 58)
The Dionne Quintuplets (born 1934, 3 still alive) (p. 58)
David Suzuki (1936–) (p. 61)
Jean Augustine (1937–) (p. 57)
Marilyn Bell (1937–) (p. 49)
Margaret Atwood (1939–) (p. 57)
Nancy Greene (1943–) (p. 53)
Joni Mitchell (1943–) (p. 60)
Roberta Bondar (1945–) (p. 19)
Marc Garneau (1949–) (p. 19)

James Gosling (1956–) (p. 59)
Rick Hansen (1957–) (p. 7)
Terry Fox (1958–1981) (p. 6)
Michael J. Fox (1961–) (p. 58)
Wayne Gretzky (1961–) (p. 48)
Jim Carrey (1962–) (p. 57)
Mike Myers (1963–) (p. 57)
Silken Laumann (1964–) (p. 53)
Céline Dion (1968–) (p. 34)
David Pelletier (1974–) (p. 49)
Jamie Salé (1977–) (p. 49)
Craig Kielburger (1982–) (p. 7)

1896–99	Klondike gold rush
1898	Yukon Territory created
1899–1902	South African (Boer) War

1900

1905	Alberta and Saskatchewan become provinces
1906	First radio voice broadcast
1914–18	World War I
1916	Manitoba, Saskatchewan and Alberta give women the vote
1917	Battle of Vimy Ridge
1918	Women get the vote in federal elections
1920	Group of Seven hold first show
1921	Banting and Best discover how to make insulin
1923	Canada wins its first Nobel Prize
1929–39	Great Depression
1929	Persons Case won by the Famous Five
1939–45	World War II

1950

1965	Canada gets its Maple Leaf flag
1966	Medical Care Act (medicare) passed
1967	Canada's Centennial year
1969	Official Languages Act passed
1970	The October Crisis
1976	Parti Québécois elected in Quebec
1982	The Charter of Rights and Freedoms and Constitution Act become law
1999	New territory of Nunavut is formed

Index